Nigeria

Since the country gained independence from the United Kingdom in 1960, Nigeria has existed in a state of permanent crisis. Dependence on oil has bound together a divided country – albeit one in which 'national unity is an obsession' – eroded its institutions and its economic and social development while leaving a legacy of corruption, coups and environmental disasters. In many respects, matters have not improved since the advent of democracy in 1999; after a spike due to the pandemic, it is estimated that 100 million Nigerians, or roughly half the population, now live below the breadline. The most disturbing aspect is the widespread violence that afflicts the country, from the terrorists of Boko Haram to the new armed separatist movements and the scourge of kidnappings, which affect ever-growing numbers of victims and from which no one is safe. How does one live in a country in which the state is at best absent, where the power is down six months of the year, public health and education are non-existent and the army is deployed in every one of the thirty-six states that make up the federation but is unable to contain the violence? Against this backdrop, the only possible option is a 'DIY' society that pops up where it can. As soon as the glimmer of an opportunity arises, Nigerians unleash all their pent-up dynamism and entrepreneurship to come up with solutions: finance apps to overcome the inaccessibility of the banking system, a solar-energy revolution to free them from the public power network – but also homespun (and polluting) methods of refining oil – e-commerce businesses using Instagram to sell traditional aphrodisiacs, films shot on tiny budgets, books and music that have taken the world by storm. No other country in Africa has such exuberant energy. And, now that the generation of generals that won the civil war and went on to govern the country for sixty years is in its twilight years, there are glimmers of hope in the refusal of increasing numbers of young people to look the other way in the face of injustice and violence – whether perpetrated by the state or otherwise. Perhaps these more vital forces will be able to take their country's future in hand – and deploy their customary ingenuity to make it work.

1

Contents

The photographs in this issue were taken by **Etinosa Yvonne**, a documentary photographer and visual artist born and bred in Nigeria. Her work focuses mainly on themes linked to the human condition and social injustice. She has received grants from the Women Photograph programme and from Art X, as well as from *National Geographic* in partnership with Lagos Photo and the Royal Photographic Society for her project 'It's All in My Head', which explores how survivors of terrorism and conflict in Nigeria cope with the fallout from their ordeals. Yvonne was one of the six individuals chosen for the 2020 cycle of World Press Photo's 6x6 Global Talent Program in Africa. Her works have been exhibited at festivals, museums and galleries in many different locations across the world.

Above: The palace historian of the Emir of Zaria, Kaduna State, poses for a portrait.
Right: Racheal Adejumo in an empty building near her home in Kaduna State. Adejumo was one of nearly forty students kidnapped by armed gunmen in Afaka, Kaduna, in March 2021. They were later released and reunited with their families.

Some Numbers

OIL ADDICTION

GDP of OPEC countries in Africa and the price of oil

GDP: billions of dollars   Price of oil: dollars per barrel
                                   on 30 June in each year

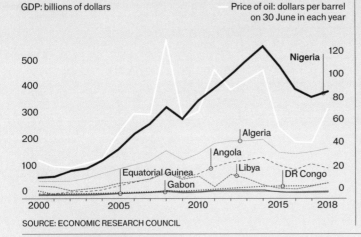

SOURCE: ECONOMIC RESEARCH COUNCIL

PLENTY IN RESERVE

Oil reserves in Africa, millions of barrels, 2021

Libya	48.4
Nigeria	36.9
Algeria	12.2
Angola	7.8
Sudan	5
Egypt	3.3
Rep. of the Congo	2.9
Uganda	2.5
Gabon	2
Chad	1.5

SOURCE: STATISTA

TROUBLED WATERS

Pirate attacks (successful and attempted) in selected territories, by country, 2020

Nigeria	35
Indonesia	26
Singapore Strait	23
Benin	11
Ghana	9
Peru	8
Philippines	8

SOURCE: STATISTA

WELL RECOMMENDED

Best African cities for a startup, 2021

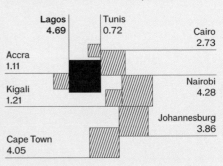

Lagos 4.69
Tunis 0.72
Cairo 2.73
Accra 1.11
Kigali 1.21
Nairobi 4.28
Johannesburg 3.86
Cape Town 4.05

The scores, calculated by the research centre StartupBlink, are based on the number and quality of the startups and other economic indicators

SOURCE: STATISTA

IN THE FAST LANE

Population of Nigeria according to the UN, millions

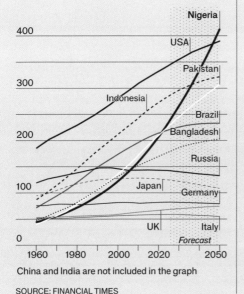

China and India are not included in the graph

SOURCE: FINANCIAL TIMES

LIKE MUSHROOMS

Cities with the highest population growth rates in the world

Gwagwalada (Nigeria) 6.46%

Kabinda (DR Congo) 6.37%

Rupganj (Bangladesh) 6.36%

Lokoja (Nigeria) 5.93%

Uige (Angola) 5.92%

SOURCE: VISUAL CAPITALIST

NOT A LOT

0.6%

of the Nigerian population are immigrants

SOURCE: STATISTA

HOMEOWNERS

25%

of Nigerians own the home in which they live, one of the lowest percentages anywhere

SOURCE: WIKIPEDIA

WORLD CITIES

Populations of the largest urban agglomerations in Africa, thousands

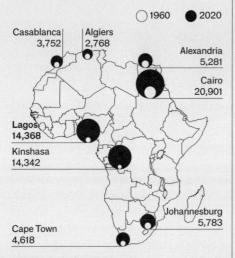

○ 1960 ● 2020

Casablanca 3,752
Algiers 2,768
Alexandria 5,281
Cairo 20,901
Lagos 14,368
Kinshasa 14,342
Johannesburg 5,783
Cape Town 4,618

SOURCE: FINANCIAL TIMES

CINEPHILES

Film industries compared, 2015

■ Nollywood □ Bollywood ▨ Hollywood

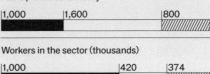

Films produced annually
1,000 1,600 800

Workers in the sector (thousands)
1,000 420 374

Income from the sector (millions of $)
590 10,900
1,500

Average budget (millions of $)
0.04 47.7
1.5

SOURCE: VICE.COM

Naija

CHIARA PIAGGIO

Translated by Alan Thawley

If there is one thing that Nigerians are really good at, it is complaining – about the government, the streets, criminality, everything – and they have excellent grounds for doing so. Living in Nigeria can be frustrating, but the country also excels in so many areas and has a wealth of potential, and young people understand this. When, in October 2020, the #EndSARS Twitter campaign against police violence (specifically against the Special Anti-Robbery Squad, or SARS) brought about the largest youth protest that Nigeria has ever seen, there was a tangible desire to build the framework of a new country, one focused on excellence, innovation and creativity. A utopia in which anything could be possible, even an end to the endless blackouts and the

jubilant cries of 'Up NEPA!' (referring to the National Electric Power Authority) when the lights finally do come back on.

This utopia has a name: Naija.

Naija is the Pidgin term used by younger people to refer to Nigeria, but what they actually mean is its opposite: Nigeria is the old country; Naija the new. Nigeria is a run-down mess, whereas Naija is a utopia. It encapsulates the fabled national optimism, the energetic interaction between strangers who feel connected at first glance by being *Naija*.

The country's vast numbers of young people (140 million are under thirty-five years old in a country of just over 200 million) have built an identity around this word. In the attempt to turn their backs on corruption, bribery and fraud they have distanced themselves from the old leadership (literally old: in 2022 the average age of the forty-four serving ministers was sixty-one) to identify instead with the dynamism of the many Nigerians

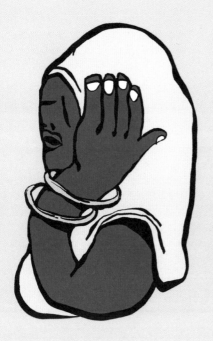

who have conquered the world with their literature, music and cinema.

And yet the term is not a new one. It comes from Pidgin English, a language born from the first contacts with Europeans as a mixture of English and local West African languages – or, as some have quipped, a language for people in a hurry who lack the time to enunciate all the syllables in a word! So 'I beg your pardon' becomes 'abeg', 'don't kill me' 'no kee me' and Nigeria, Naija. Still too long? The most pressed for time can simply write '9ja'. Nowadays Pidgin charts its own course and is no longer simply a contact language but a creole, a second, unofficial language that can be used in institutional contexts such as TV and radio – the BBC even has a dedicated Pidgin news service. And the term Naija has also changed direction. Once used as an exclamation to express irritation – 'Traffic jam! *Naijaaa!*' – it entered youth slang in the 2000s, spreading first on the streets of

Lagos and then on social media, in songs, in Nollywood films, advertising campaigns and the hashtags of millions of posts.

And so it became a symbol for another Nigeria, where young people are finally united in this country of three hundred ethnicities and five hundred languages all bundled up together within the same arbitrary borders during the colonial era: the shop assistant who sells water sachets in the evenings in the rumbling traffic of Oshodi, the new graduate setting up a digital business in a remote location, the unemployed youth who survives as best he can – young men and women excluded from institutional political and economic power but busy writing the history of a new country with flamboyant self-assurance.

In essence, Naija is about patriotism from the bottom up, young people laying claim to an identity in their own image, breaking away from the past. And this is perhaps what really drives its use: Nigeria is the name given to them by the British, but Naija is entirely Nigerian. An endonym that exudes awareness. A noun that can become an adjective when needed (Naija people, Naija food) but is, first and foremost, a feeling: Naija-ness.

And it is of no importance that the older generations are unable to decipher it, that they see the use of the term as a juvenile expression, the sign of a cultural decline, the habit of elevating the language of social media to the norm. Young people use it with pride, repeating a motto that is almost a mantra: Naija no dey carry last – Naija will never come last.

And so a question presents itself, which seems counterintuitive, yet another paradox in this land where oxymorons converge: can you be patriotic without feeling that your country represents you? In Nigeria, yes you can.

Fetching water from a pond
in Geller, Adamawa State.

The Do-It-Yourself Society

'Every household is its own government,' people say in Nigeria, and this is reflected in virtually every aspect of public and private life. It is the key to arriving at a better understanding of this rich universe of a country.

FEMKE VAN ZEIJL
Translated by Emma Rault

11

The exhaust fumes form dense clouds above the motion-less traffic on Bodija Road. It's Saturday night, and all of Ibadan seems to be on its way somewhere. Three lines of cars have somehow managed to squeeze on to the two-lane road. When a share-taxi driver decides to nudge his beaten-up Micra out into the flow of traffic in the hope of reaching his destination more quickly, the chaos is complete. His red-and-yellow cab is faced with a honking mass of oncoming cars while the traffic behind him is already bumper-to-bumper. The result is total gridlock: no one can move either forwards or backwards. The traffic in the heart of one of Nigeria's largest cities is at a complete standstill, and the traffic cops who normally keep an eye on things from a tin shack in the middle of the confusing intersection are nowhere to be found.

Then a small miracle happens. A tall man gets out of one of the cars, walks over to the Micra and begins to reason with the stressed taxi driver. He gestures towards the cars behind him like the conductor of a symphony orchestra, and, lo and behold, they start to move. The drivers all defer to this self-appointed traffic conductor as though he were in uniform and duti-fully put their cars into reverse. Inch by inch, this member of the public success-fully clears the intersection of traffic then gets back into his own car to continue on his way.

This spontaneous initiative, instigated by a regular civilian, took place on a busy road leading to the market in Ibadan, a city more than a hundred kilometres from Lagos. But it could just as well have taken place in Kano, the northern city with a population of more than four million, during the hustle and bustle of the annual Durbar festival. Or in Enugu, in south-eastern Nigeria. Or in Port Harcourt, the oil town in the Niger Delta. Nigerians don't need the authorities to solve these kinds of everyday snags; they just take matters into their own hands.

This Nigerian DIY mindset goes way beyond dealing with a simple traffic bottleneck. Decades of indifferent and inadequate government oversight have accustomed Nigerians to being self-reliant: no one depends on public services, which are, as a rule, insufficient and some-times lacking altogether. They respond to this predicament with boundless inventiveness.

'Every household is its own govern-ment,' people say in Nigeria, and this is reflected in virtually every aspect of public and private life. It is the key to arriving at a better understanding of this rich universe of a country.

One of the most readily apparent aspects of the DIY society is the way Nigerians have to generate their own electricity. Africa's largest oil producer is only able to supply around four thousand megawatts of power to an estimated population of 180 million (although some believe it to be higher) – a tiny fraction of the national electricity demand; 43 per cent of the population is not connected to the grid, and, for those who are, frequent power outages are the norm.

When that happens, a rattling choir

FEMKE VAN ZEIJL is a Dutch writer and journalist who has been working and living in Nigeria since 2012, making her one of the longest-serving foreign correspondents in Africa's most populous country. Her fourth book, *De doe-het-zelfmaatschappij* ('Do-It-Yourself Society', Ambo|Anthos, 2022), is an in-depth study of the themes covered in this essay.

A phone-charging business
in the federal capital, Abuja.

UP NEPA!

The room is dark, lit by a few candles.
Suddenly a noise, a sort of hum. The house
reawakens, everyone rushes to turn on their
mobile phones, chargers, modems, fridges,
washing machines … The humming is the
sign that the electricity is coming back on,
and the jubilant cry of 'Up NEPA!' rings
out. NEPA stands for the National Electric
Power Authority – or, as Nigerians would
have it, 'Never Expect Power Always' – and
is synonymous with electricity. It matters
little that the government agency has long
since ceased to exist, having been absorbed
into the Power Holding Company of Nigeria,
PHCN (or 'Please Hold Candle Nearby');
NEPA remains the name of the country's
largest source of frustration (and satire).
The World Bank has calculated that the
power is down for 4,600 hours a year, or
six months, which is more than any other
African country. Electricity comes and
goes unpredictably, and blackouts can
last a few minutes, hours, days or even
months or years in some areas. While
you can get used to it at home – or buy
yourself a small petrol generator – for all
kinds of businesses the additional cost
of having to ensure your own constant
supply is disastrous for the balance sheet.
The IMF estimates that the Nigerian
economy loses $29 billion a year through
outages. There are multiple causes:
chronic lack of investment, low energy
production, insufficient maintenance,
wastage in distribution, a poorly designed
privatisation in 2014 … In the meantime,
resigned Nigerians keep their ears open
for the hum so they can shout, 'Up NEPA!'

'The roar of these generators is the soundtrack of the DIY society, and anyone visiting the country for the first time finds themselves overwhelmed by the noise and fumes of this widespread alternative power source.'

of generators starts up. There was a time when buying a generator was an impossible dream for the average Nigerian, but the advent of the five-litre generator has transformed the landscape. These low-cost power sources are popularly referred to as 'I better pass my neighbour', Nigerian Pidgin that loosely translates as 'I'm better off than my neighbour'. The tank holds about five litres of petrol mixed with oil, which will last you around five hours. It produces 750 watts, enough to power a couple of lamps, a fan and a television. Small and portable, they fit on even the narrowest balcony, and their introduction in the 1990s democratised the use of generators in Nigeria, something that had previously been the preserve of the elite. Now they're everywhere – in markets, on shopping streets and in middle-class suburbs, in the slums, out in the countryside and in camps for internally displaced people. The roar of these generators is the soundtrack of the DIY society, and anyone visiting the country for the first time finds themselves overwhelmed by the noise and fumes of this widespread alternative power source.

Because of the pollution and the high cost, however – Nigerians collectively spend an average of $21 billion on fuel for their generators every year – alternative solutions for private electricity generation are met with great enthusiasm. One example is the growing popularity of solar: the sale of solar panels has increased exponentially over the past few years, with Nigeria making its way into the top five countries in the world for sales of domestic solar power systems in 2019. More and more fancy villas and middle-class roofs are gleaming with silicon cells.

Where in Europe having solar panels on your roof might attest to environmental consciousness, and in the USA going off grid is a political statement, in Nigeria solar energy is pure necessity, a logical response to the awareness that sooner or later public services will let you down. The Nigerian people's determination to solve their own problems has transformed the country into one of the world's fastest-growing markets for solar energy.

All of which means that Nigeria may never arrive at the stage of having a nationwide power grid; instead, they may skip ahead to a more sustainable network of renewable energy. This is one way in which a clear development gap – there are few countries with worse power grids than Nigeria – can end up being a developmental advantage.

One of the reasons electricity is indispensable for the average Nigerian household is that it is needed to power their water pumps. This is because, in addition to inadequate power supplies, they are also dealing with dramatic water shortages. Only 10 per cent of Nigerians have access to tap water; it's been that way ever since colonial times.

When Lord Lugard, Nigeria's first

In the late 1990s the Dutch architect Rem Koolhaas, who ran a Harvard research programme studying urban design around the world, developed a passionate interest in Lagos, visiting around twenty times in five years and observing the transition to democracy. In the Nigerian metropolis, which at the time was not in the loop of globalised cities, Koolhaas wanted to study the modernisation of a country through one of its main drivers, urbanisation, and see what happens in a society where the state is absent. He observed countless examples of what he termed 'self-organisation', such as the markets that form spontaneously during the immense traffic jams (known to Nigerians as 'go-slows') or along the platforms where trains progress at walking pace. In a 2016 interview in the *Guardian*, he explained that 'each citizen needed to take, in any day, maybe 400 or 500 independent decisions on how to survive that extremely complex system ... it was the ultimate dysfunctional city – but actually, in terms of all the initiatives and ingenuity, it mobilised an incredibly beautiful, almost utopian landscape of independence and agency'. The project, however, was criticised as being 'neo-colonialist' and the idea of self-organisation challenged as too rosy an interpretation of the collective capacity for adaptation to extreme living conditions. The result was that Koolhaas's team never published its studies, which now survive only in the form of a documentary by the Dutch filmmaker Bregtje van der Haak available on YouTube, *Lagos/Koolhaas* (2002).

British governor-general, opened the public waterworks in Lagos in 1915, the handful of farmers in the surrounding area were told they were no longer allowed to use the two rivers that the water came from for bathing or washing – a rule that was strictly enforced by police patrols. But they weren't allowed to use the tap water either. The pipeline went straight from Iju Waterworks to Ikoyi, the island where the colonial elite lived. The cast-iron pipe that travelled thirty-five kilometres from the mainland didn't detour through a single one of the villages it passed along the way, and the local population remained dependent on wells and natural sources.

In the 21st century there are still neighbourhoods in Africa's biggest city where the residents have never – at any point in history – had access to tap water. And the limited plumbing system that is in place never expanded to keep pace with the population, which means the water constantly sputters to a halt. Even being hooked up to 'government water', as Nigerians call tap water, comes with no guarantee.

What's true for Lagos is true for all of Nigeria. In Maiduguri, the city in the north-east that has ended up becoming overpopulated following an influx of people fleeing the Boko Haram violence in the region, half of all households have to depend on their own supplies of water. And, in some neighbourhoods in the southern city of Uyo, water stopped coming out of the taps years ago. Even the residents of Abuja, Nigeria's centrally located capital, which was constructed in the 1980s, frequently find themselves without water.

It's no wonder, then, that the DIY approach is widespread in this arena, too. If there is no water-supply network in the vicinity or the government water isn't running, Nigerians will simply dig a well

Above: A generator used to provide electricity to shops in Bayelsa State.
Opposite: Pumping water from a well in Zaria, Kaduna State.

on their property, install a pump or build a giant water-storage structure. The skyline of virtually every Nigerian city has become dotted with black, blue and green water tanks that protrude above the rooftops and attest to the self-sufficiency of every household.

Those who lack the funds – DIY strategies are rarely cheap – can always turn to the *maruwa*, young men who push carts down the streets stacked with as many as twenty fifty-litre jerry cans of water and sell them at an affordable price. Usually, these water vendors are from the northern part of the country, which is how they got their name: *mai* means 'owner' and *ruwa* 'water' in Hausa, the lingua franca of northern Nigeria. They demonstrate one of the universal rules of the DIY society: the moment a public service disappears, entrepreneurs will rise up to fill the gap.

But some gaps are more easily filled than others. While individual households can take care of their own power and water supplies with some creativity and effort, when it comes to education and healthcare things are a lot more complicated. And in these sectors, too, public services across the country are falling phenomenally short. In 2020 less than 5 per cent of the government budget was allocated to

healthcare, which means that in that year Nigeria only spent about five dollars per capita on public health. Six per cent of the federal budget went to education, which is far below the 15–20 per cent recommended by UNESCO, the United Nations agency tasked with promoting international cooperation in the fields of education, science and culture. That's why anyone who can even remotely afford it avoids the chronically underfunded public sector. It's no surprise that private schools and private clinics are popping up all over the place.

Here we do see a stark difference between the north and the south. In the desert-like, socio-economically disadvantaged north, few people have the means to escape the dysfunctional public sector. There, the lack of decent state schools and hospitals is reflected in high illiteracy rates – in some northern states, fewer than 10 per cent of the population can read and write – and a grim world record in child mortality: one in five children will die before reaching their fifth birthday.

Self-sufficiency is a privilege; it's not an option for everyone.

The DIY society not only widens the gap between rich and poor it also makes the richest all but independent of public services. After all, for the elite there's always going abroad as the ultimate escape strategy. Those who can afford it send their children to universities in the USA, the UK, Cyprus or one of the Caribbean islands and will travel to India, Turkey or any other country with a more robust healthcare system for medical treatment. Even the president of Nigeria gets on a plane and checks himself into a London clinic the moment he's faced with a health issue.

'Many Nigerians have long since stopped feeling like stakeholders in their own society. If every household is its own government, why bother with the national government at all?'

This means that the elite that runs the country can get their needs met elsewhere, while the poor who are left behind end up suffering most from the inadequate public infrastructure.

What kind of society do we see when such a large proportion of households are essentially left to fend for themselves? Self-sufficiency comes at a price; many Nigerians have long since stopped feeling like stakeholders in their own society. If every household is its own government, why bother with the national government at all?

The golden rule of the DIY society is a tacit agreement between citizens and the political sphere to stay out of each other's way. Citizens rarely hold politicians accountable for the billions they put into their own pockets; in return, the government doesn't hassle private citizens by trying to enforce rules, taxes or other inconveniences.

This live-and-let-live pact can only exist in Nigeria because the majority of the government's income doesn't derive from its private citizens. About two-thirds of the public budget is funded by the revenue from crude oil from the Niger Delta – free money that no one has to account for. But with the role of fossil fuels set to decline in the future and the need for alternative government income streams becoming increasingly pressing, the pact is coming under pressure. The authorities are increasingly trying to impose their will on the public, but people aren't used to government intervention and aren't prepared to give up their de facto free state.

The question is how the Nigerian government can win back its legitimacy and regain public trust, especially since the very same government has been systematically promoting the DIY mentality for decades. There's the state of Oyo, for example, which tells school boards to fund their budgets with gifts from wealthy alumni; there's the Lagos State commissioner for energy and mineral resources encouraging the wealthy to buy solar panels to take pressure off the grid; and there's the Nigerian Army, which, in its fight against Boko Haram, works closely with civil militias. These are just a few examples of how the authorities actively promote private initiative.

On top of this, the DIY mentality has permeated the government apparatus itself. The ubiquitous corruption is nothing more than bringing that same survival strategy for daily life into the workings of government. 'Anything for the boys?' police officers will routinely ask from inside their

A wooden bridge in Okuto, Bayelsa State, funded and built by a private citizen. Prior to the construction of this walkway, the community was only accessible by a much longer and more circuitous route.

checkpoints, in the hope of supplementing their meagre salaries with anything they are able to extort from private citizens. And civil servants take advantage of the slow wheels of government bureaucracy by offering fast-track services: for a fee they will expedite getting your passport, driving licence or marriage certificate processed. They have figured out a way to game the dysfunctional system to their advantage, which is typical of the DIY society.

It's not just ordinary Nigerians who do this but also those in the upper echelons of politics. Take a career politician like Bola Tinubu, the former governor of Lagos State. When his second and final term in office was nearing its end, one of the last things he did was to implement a new pension law for former governors. In addition to continuing to receive the same salary as the incumbent, he also allotted himself a house in Abuja and another in Lagos, six cars that are to be replaced every three years, a brand-new suite of furniture

every two years, a cook, steward, gardener and other domestic staff and free medical treatment, all of which is funded by Lagos State. Pushing through new legislation providing for your retirement right before you're thrown to the wolves in a country with no social safety net – now there's an effective do-it-yourself approach.

But the DIY hacks devised by enterprising citizens don't necessarily have to be a burden on the rest of society. Sometimes that very self-sufficiency actually ends up creating a solution to a society-wide problem. Take the opening scene of this essay, in which a private citizen appointed himself as a makeshift traffic controller and was single-handedly able to untangle a jam. This is emblematic of the widespread Nigerian capacity for informal mediation. It's not only in traffic that Nigerians reveal themselves to be highly skilled at defusing conflict; on other occasions, too, they demonstrate a remarkable ability to

THE PASSENGER   Femke van Zeijl

In the world of start-ups, unicorns are private companies valued at more than a billion dollars, and a few years ago Nigeria became the first African country to boast unicorns of its own. The fact that they are exclusively *financial* start-ups is no big surprise: when less than half of the population has a bank account (because the banks are not reliable, too far away – given the size of the country – or expensive), apps step in to fill the gap. The result is that the largest of them, like Flutterwave or Interswitch, are worth as much as the traditional banks themselves, and more and more banking services are supplied by intermediaries, who find it easy to obtain a licence and a payment terminal. So while electronic payments are growing at a dizzying pace in Nigeria, the unicorns are investing millions in marketing to get product endorsements from local celebrities. And yet there appears to be little in the way of guaranteed growth: the population is getting poorer, and financial and banking regulations change rapidly and apparently arbitrarily. Analysts wonder how long the boom will last. But, while the financial sector attracts the most investments and generates the highest returns, it is not the only domain in which start-ups are active; in the DIY society there is one for practically everything. Alongside the #EndSARS movement's protests, the first apps for personal security emerged, featuring colour-coded panic buttons to be activated depending on the type of danger. These alert family members of the person under threat and, in some cases, other subscribers to the app in the vicinity. If people cannot rely on their institutions, they have to put their faith in one another.

de-escalate a situation when tempers are running high.

This tendency to keep the peace is ingrained in the Nigerian mentality and stems partly from the traditional way that many ethnic groups in Nigeria resolved their conflicts long before the colonisers arrived. Back then it was the elders in the community who settled local disputes and weighed the interests of society against those of the individual. They preferred to come to a verdict that everyone was happy with – a verdict that was accepted because of the natural authority their senior role afforded them. Nowadays people often fall back on these kinds of traditional authorities, even reinventing them if needs be, simply because it's a much quicker way out of an impasse than taking things to court.

These types of alternative conflict mediators can even be found in the cultural melting pot that is Lagos. Near the University of Lagos campus, for example, you will find Baba Osho, a man in his eighties who once came to the big city to help his uncle but amassed such a huge fortune that he grew to be one of the most respected people in his neighbourhood. His wealth and age lent him authority, and now locals turn to him when they find themselves at loggerheads. Baba Osho will sit them down at his kitchen table so they can figure things out. The reason this works is because no one wants to get stuck in the country's corrupt judicial system; trials often drag on for decades and cost a fortune in legal fees. The average Nigerian is all too aware that it's better to resolve a dispute without intervention from the authorities, which

Opposite: Tuebi Sapere-obi, who funded and built the wooden bridge in the photograph on page 19.

will only cost time and money. As a result, unpaid peacemakers like Baba Osho can be found all over the country. Scuffles on the street are broken up by passers-by; arguments in the market are settled by the woman who is traditionally in charge; disputes between neighbours are resolved by the retired teacher who lives across the street. In many of these cases, someone will volunteer themselves for the role of peacemaker – usually a man, sometimes an older woman.

But there is a thin line between informal conflict mediation and vigilante justice, or 'jungle justice' as Nigerians call it. There are no reliable statistics available as to the prevalence of lynchings in the country. In a 2014 survey, 42 per cent of respondents stated they had witnessed such acts of mob justice at some point. Even being accused of something as minor as petty theft at the market can come at a high price – a few hotheads in the crowd, a stray car tyre and a splash of petrol can all too easily turn a mere scuffle into a lynching.

In short, Nigerians consider informal conflict mediation an acceptable alternative to the official justice system, and, in principle, this could take some of the strain off the backlogged courts, but, like all DIY solutions, this one, too, has its downside.

Nigerian society is far from unique when it comes to the self-sufficiency its citizens are forced to embrace. In fact, the DIY society is the norm worldwide and the northern-European welfare state the exception. And you'd be wrong to assume Nigerians are less inclined by nature to look for community-wide solutions – if circumstances allow – than people in other parts of the world. In spite of everything, they try for it time and again.

In October 2020 thousands of young

YAHOO BOYS

'When the son of the deposed king of Nigeria emails you directly asking for help, you help!' shouts the officer manager in the American version of the TV series *The Office*, a regular victim of online scams. This 'Nigerian prince' scam that has now become a feature of TV plotlines follows a pattern: the alleged holder of a bank account containing a vast sum of money (often a deposed prince) asks for some minor financial assistance to unblock the funds, promising a handsome reward in return. Once the sum required to unblock the account is paid, however, he disappears. In Nigeria the crime is covered by a specific section of the penal code, and yet becoming a Yahoo Boy (as the fraudsters are known) is an occupation like any other and can even be quite lucrative. It all began in the 1990s with the spread of internet cafés. The scammers, who at the time were mostly comparatively uneducated, earned little from their attempts to swindle the odd sucker, but the second wave of Yahoo Boys was different: these were young people trained in IT who, disillusioned by the lack of jobs, tried to pull off scams worth millions. The fact that they are now apparently wealthy and respected figures makes the 'profession' even more attractive, even to the point of paradox. One striking case was that of Obinwanne Okeke, who was arrested for defrauding a UK company of millions in 2018, not so much because of the sum he stole but because Okeke was a respected businessman who had appeared on the cover of *Forbes Africa* and taught at the London School of Economics. He was topping up his salary with online scams, a way of relieving huge companies of a small portion of their profits, almost like a modern-day Robin Hood.

has no idea what to do with a generation of protesting digital citizens who turn to the internet for information and communication, and so it responds with violence – the last resort of a regime that has lost its legitimacy.

On the evening of 20 October 2020 the Nigerian military opened fire on the peaceful protesters in Lagos, resulting in dozens of casualties and several deaths. This put a swift end to the demonstrations, but the fire of change keeps burning on social media, fuelled by the experiences shared by the young protesters during the uprisings, particularly in the south. During the two weeks of protests, from Kaduna to Calabar and from Osogbo to Owerri, they had showed in microcosm how to organise a society. The protesters nominated people to act as stewards and maintain order, shared the contact information of lawyers online who were on standby if anyone was arrested, shared meals and first-aid kits, and volunteers swept the streets afterwards. The protesters were the first to point out that they were doing, on all kinds of levels, what their own government was failing to do. This was what Nigerian society could look like.

This is how Nigeria's youngest generation and largest demographic came to realise that there is an alternative to the DIY society, one from which everyone stands to benefit. Whether the political sphere will ever catch up remains to be seen, but if the government were able to step up to the plate, even just a little bit more, together with the self-sufficiency and entrepreneurial spirit of the population this would make an unbeatable combination. Were we to see this kind of shift take place, Nigeria would become an economic force to be reckoned with. 🖋

Nigerians took to the streets for the first time in years. They were demonstrating against the Special Anti-Robbery Squad (SARS), a police unit notorious for committing acts of torture and other unlawful practices with impunity, especially against young men. The protests used the hashtag #EndSARS, but they were about much more than police brutality. Young Nigerians are fed up with the marginalisation, disenfranchisement and lack of economic prospects that characterise their lives in the DIY society.

It turned into a real clash between generations. The Nigerian population is one of the youngest in the world, yet the incumbent president at the time of writing is eighty years old, and the average age of the ministers is sixty-one. The country is run by a gerontocracy rooted in a military tradition. This government

Nigeria and Its Military: Between a Rock and a Hard Place

A girl removes campaign posters from a wall in Awka, Anambra State, a few days ahead of the election for governor.

The generation of army generals who won the Nigerian Civil War in the 1960s has dominated politics ever since. While they have long been regarded as the architects of national unity, their interference has also provoked anger among the population. Although those who remain are now heading towards retirement, the ongoing influence of these ex-soldiers remains a controversial subject.

MAX SIOLLUN

25

Nigeria is a country of many contradictions. It is a divided country in which national unity is an obsession and a rich country with millions of poor people.

As in the USA, Israel and Turkey, Nigeria is a country in which the military has played a huge role in shaping the nation's identity. Unlike the first three, though, Nigeria's soldiers are not viewed as heroes by most of their compatriots; they are, instead, disliked and stereotyped as aggressive troublemakers and human-rights abusers. Yet, even though Nigerians would be loath to admit it, there are few nations where the fate of a country and its military are so intertwined as in Nigeria. Throughout the country's sixty-two years as an independent nation, two of its most incendiary controversies have been the relationship between the military and politics and the relationship between the state and the hundreds of ethnic groups within it. The military has been at the forefront of addressing these issues. For more than six decades Nigeria has tried a cocktail of solutions with different ingredients to deal with these two challenges, but in 2023 one of the key cocktail ingredients will be removed after President Buhari (a retired army general) completes his second and final term of office in May.

Nigeria is Africa's richest and most populous country. Its 2020 gross domestic product (GDP) of approximately $450 billion per year is slightly larger than that of Austria and slightly smaller than Belgium's. Nigeria's GDP is greater than the combined GDPs of its fourteen neighbouring members of the Economic Community of West African States. The United Nations estimates that by 2050 Nigeria will be the third-most populous nation in the world, behind only China and India, with a population of 400 million.

'THE MOST COMPLICATED COUNTRY IN THE WORLD'

Governing Nigeria is no easy task. It is one of the most ethnically and linguistically diverse countries in the world, and its many ethnic, linguistic, religious and social cleavages are so complex and voluminous that the American professor John Paden described it as 'the most complicated country in the world' during a United States Institute for Peace event. It has more than 300 ethnic groups and over 520 different languages. The three largest ethnic groups are the Hausa, who are mainly Muslim and live in the north of the country, the Igbo, who are mainly Christians and live in the south-east, and the Yoruba, who live in the south-west and roughly half of whom are Muslim and the other half Christian, making Nigeria the

MAX SIOLLUN is one of Nigeria's most important historians, who has written extensively on the history of Nigeria's military. His latest book, *What Britain Did to Nigeria: A Short History of Conquest and Rule* (Hurst, 2021), is a study of Nigeria under British colonial rule and the legacy of that period.

'The coup was meant to be a brief and temporary revolution to fight corruption and disorder. The "temporary" military solution lasted for decades.'

only country in the world with its population split equally between Christians and Muslims. The fact that Muslims live predominantly in the north and Christians predominantly in the south also adds a geographical polarisation to religious controversies.

Contemporary Nigeria cannot be understood without reference to its past. After independence from Britain in 1960, the cultural, geographical, numerical and developmental differences between the north and south fuelled each region's fear of domination by the other. The south was more economically and educationally advanced than the north. Igbos especially benefited from the massive educational disparity between north and south and, after the departure of the British, migrated north to fill the administrative and technical jobs vacated by departing colonial officers. This migration stoked fear among northerners that they would be economically and educationally dominated by the better-educated southerners and by Igbos in particular. Southerners, in their turn, were apprehensive that the north's numerical majority in the Federal Parliament would lead to permanent northern political domination of the country. These mutually enforcing fears paralysed the country's politics and generated numerous political crises.

MILITARY RULE
On 15 January 1966 a group of young, idealistic, socialist army officers (many of whom trained at Britain's elite Royal Military Academy Sandhurst) forcibly broke the political deadlock by overthrowing the government in a violent military coup. Although most of Nigeria's current population had not been born when that coup occurred, its consequences continue to haunt the country today. It was meant to be a brief and temporary revolution to fight corruption and disorder. The 'temporary' military solution lasted for decades, as eight different military governments ruled Nigeria for twenty-nine of the next thirty-three years.

The manner in which the coup was conducted coincided with and amplified existing conflict cleavages. The coup leaders were mostly Igbo Christians from the south. Several of their victims were northerners. The coup leaders assassinated the prime minister, Sir Abubakar Tafawa Balewa, and the premier of the Northern Region, Sir Ahmadu Bello, both of whom were Muslims. Northerners were outraged at the murder of their leaders and interpreted the coup as an Igbo-led conspiracy to subjugate the north and impose Igbo dominance. Six months later northern soldiers staged another, even bloodier, revenge coup against their Igbo colleagues. Less than six years after independence, factions in the multi-ethnic army, which had been heralded as the only truly national institution in a divided country, turned their guns on each other. More violence followed the two coups as northern mobs killed 30,000 Igbos in late 1966, and Igbos escaped back to their homeland in the south-east. Less than a year later, in May 1967, the south-east of the country seceded from Nigeria and formed a new breakaway state, Biafra. Britain armed and supported the northern-led Nigerian federal army in its campaign to reintegrate Biafra into Nigeria by force. Almost three years of brutal civil war followed, and for the first time presented Western television viewers with the now-stereotypical images of emaciated and starving African children. The Nigerian military imposed a land, air and sea blockade that starved Biafra into surrender in January 1970. Nigeria reabsorbed Biafra after its leaders promised to be 'loyal Nigerian citizens' once again.

THE BROTHERS' WAR
Two of Nigeria's greatest ironies are that it had to fight a war and break apart in order to come together and that a civil war created a consensus for national unity. Rather than mete out punishment for the secession, as Igbos had feared and dreaded, the extremely magnanimous wartime leader Major-General Yakubu Gowon said in an interview in *Time* magazine in 1969: 'We do not take the Igbos as our enemies; they are our brothers.' He surprisingly declared that the war's end was 'the dawn of national reconciliation' and that there would be 'no victor, no vanquished'. He proclaimed a general amnesty for combatants on both sides, refused to hold war-crimes trials or to punish either those who led the secession or those who suppressed it. He also declined to award medals to any soldiers who fought in the war, as it was deemed dishonourable to reap reward from fighting one's brothers. Some Biafran soldiers were even allowed to rejoin the post-war Nigerian army. The Igbos were to be treated as returning prodigal sons and daughters rather than as defeated

enemies. This was the high point of national unity. Outsiders were so astonished at the remarkable reconciliation that a British journalist, John De St. Jorre, wrote in his book *The Brothers' War*: 'it may be that when history takes a longer view of Nigeria's war, it will be shown that while the black man has little to teach us about making war he has a real contribution to offer in making peace'.

A NATION BUILT IN ITS MILITARY'S IMAGE
After the Brothers' War Gowon also said that 'We have the opportunity to build a new nation.' The 1966 coups and civil war propelled a group of young military officers on to the national political stage. Using their esteem as victorious war commanders, they restructured Nigeria to ensure that it would never again break apart or fight another civil war.

They repeatedly sub-divided the country into thirty-six states and funded the states, thereby creating a financial disincentive against another secession. They also promulgated a new constitution in 1979, which introduced a new concept of 'federal character', an affirmative-action programme that requires the composition of the government to 'reflect the federal character of Nigeria'. Its purpose was to ensure that no ethnic group could monopolise leadership of the government or be excluded from national economic and political opportunities. The constitution even forbids political parties from using any names, logos or mottoes with ethnic, geographical or religious connotations and bans them if their membership does not satisfy constitutional diversity requirements.

By the time military rule ended in 1999, the young twenty- and thirty-something civil-war-era army officers who redesigned Nigeria were millionaire

Above: #EndSARS protesters march down one of Abuja's busiest streets.
Below: A woman searches for her name on her ward's voters' register in the capital during the presidential election.

'By the time military rule ended in 1999, the young civil-war-era army officers who redesigned Nigeria were millionaire grandfathers in their sixties.'

grandfathers in their sixties. They interfered in the transition from military to civilian rule, engineered what the civilian opposition criticised, in the words of musician Fela Kuti, as an 'army arrangement' and ensured that Nigeria's new democratically elected president in 1999 was a retired army officer, General Olusegun Obasanjo, who had previously led a military government. Obasanjo (then a colonel) had been the officer to whom Biafra's army surrendered when the civil war ended in 1970.

Most Nigerians dislike the political meddling of the retired generals; however, although they would never admit it, the retired generals' experience has been essential in mediating crises. Even when a retired general is not the president, the military finds a way to shape political outcomes. The only democratic transfer of power from one civilian government to another occurred in 2015 after General Obasanjo publicly rebuked and withdrew support from the incumbent, President Goodluck Jonathan. Another former military ruler, General Abdulsalami Abubakar, helped to pre-empt a crisis by visiting the presidential villa to convince Jonathan to concede and accept the results of an election that some of Jonathan's ruling party members had vowed to challenge in court. The influence of retired military officers caused a realignment of political forces that led to the election of another retired military officer as president, Major-General Muhammadu Buhari.

However, the retired generals should also take the blame for creating the conditions for two of Nigeria's most serious current problems: insecurity and economic inequality. Their fixation on keeping Nigeria together, by force if necessary, has led to a near-obsessive ethnic micro-management of national life. They implemented federal character in a way that turned Nigeria into a nation that exists almost simply to share money and jobs. An ethnic quota regulates just about every facet of public life, such as admission to the government and into the civil service. Even schools, universities, the military and the police regulate recruitment by regional origin.

However, the hyper-vigilance on ethnic sharing of national opportunities and resources became, ironically, a source of disunity. The states with fewer educationally and professionally qualified people defended the federal character, while states with too many for their quota attacked it. The latter group claim that it sacrifices merit, and because of it 'the public service became a dumping ground for incompetent, ill-motivated servants from different parts of the country', as reported in the *Guardian* (Lagos) in 2006.

Eleven of the fifteen governments in Nigeria's history have been led by serving or retired military officers. They continued to preach the post-civil-war gospel of national unity long after they needed to and failed to recognise that Nigeria's modern political conversation has turned away from whether the country should remain united to a shades-of-grey consideration of what national unity means. Military governments ignored

Independent Nigeria: The first six decades

1956

After fifty years of fruitless exploration, the first oilfield is discovered in Nigeria, in Oloibiri in the Niger Delta.

1960

On 1 October Nigeria becomes an independent country, as a federation of three regions (Northern, Western and Eastern). The first post-colonial national government is led by Prime Minister Sir Abubakar Tafawa Balewa, a northerner. Major disparities in terms of economic development and the education system spark tensions between the country's three largest ethnic groups (Hausa, Yoruba and Igbo).

1966

In January, in the first of a long series of coups, Tafawa Balewa is assassinated by a group of Igbo army officers. A counter-coup led by northern officers in July leads to the installation of the then Lieutenant-Colonel (later Major-General) Yakubu Gowon as head of state. As a result of the ensuing massacre of thousands of Igbo people in the north of the country, a million of them flee to the Eastern Region, igniting separatist sentiments.

1967

Lieutenant-Colonel Emeka Ojukwu declares independence for the Eastern Region (including the Niger Delta and its oil reserves) under the name of the Republic of Biafra. The writer Chinua Achebe becomes the new state's ambassador. A bloody civil war ensues, ending with the defeat of Biafra in 1970.

1970

The musician Fela Kuti founds the Kalakuta Republic, a commune that declares independence from the military government, holding out until 1978.

1975

Following a period of reconciliation aided by an economic boom after a surge in oil prices, Gowon, accused of delaying the promised return to civilian government, is overthrown by Murtala Mohammed, who is, in turn, assassinated the following year in a failed coup. His second-in-command, Olusegun Obasanjo, continues the process of economic diversification and transition towards an American-style presidential constitution. Planning for the transfer of the federal capital to Abuja, a new city in the centre of the country, begins.

1979

The former finance minister and director of the Central Bank of Nigeria, Shehu Shagari, is elected as the first president of the Second Republic. Under the motto 'One nation, one destiny', Nigeria makes great progress in education, agriculture and women's participation in public life, but corruption is rife.

1983

Despite the collapse in oil prices, Shagari wins a second term amid violence and accusations of electoral fraud. On 31 December he is deposed by General Muhammadu Buhari, who remains in power for two years (during which time he has his opponent Fela Kuti arrested) before himself being replaced by another general, Ibrahim Badamasi Babangida (aka IBB), in 1985.

(The country had not seen the last of Buhari, however.) The second half of the 1980s is blighted by corruption and economic crisis, but IBB begins a (slow) return to civilian rule, delayed, among other things, by a failed coup in 1990. In 1986 Wole Soyinka wins the Nobel Prize for Literature.

1993

The free, democratic elections are won by the businessman M.K.O. Abiola, a Yoruba Muslim from the south, with a supporter base that cuts across different ethnic groups and regions, but the Third Republic never sees the light of day after IBB annuls the result, causing a political crisis that leads to a coup led by yet another general, Sani Abacha, who installs a brutal dictatorship. Abiola is arrested in 1994 (he dies in prison in 1998 in circumstances that have yet to be explained) and to this day remains a symbol of Nigerian democracy. This same year Abiola's supporter Wole Soyinka flees the country on a motorbike and is sentenced to death *in absentia*.

1995

The military junta arrests former head of state Olusegun Obasanjo on the grounds of alleged support for a plot. The writer Ken Saro-Wiwa is hanged after a sham trail, along with another eight Ogoni activists. In response, Nigeria is suspended from the Commonwealth of Nations and sanctions are imposed by the United States and the European Union.

1998

Abacha dies suddenly; his replacement Abdulsalami Abubakar begins the transition to a civilian rule. The following year Obasanjo, released from prison just a few months previously, wins the presidential

election, signalling the start of the Fourth Republic, which has yet to be superseded.

2000

A number of states in the north adopt sharia law as their legal system. Ethnic and religious tensions result in several massacres and repression on the part of the army. Around a hundred people are killed in Lagos in 2002 in clashes between Hausa and Yoruba. This same year, in Kaduna, protests by Muslims against the Miss World beauty pageant lead to a further two hundred deaths, and the event is moved to London.

2003

Obasanjo is voted in for a second term, in spite of serious irregularities in the voting. He appoints Ngozi Okonjo-Iweala finance minister, making her the first woman to hold the position. Inter-ethnic massacres continue, and in 2004 clashes begin in the south as well – bloodily repressed by the army – with attacks on oil pipelines and kidnappings of foreign oil-company employees. The first Nigerian satellite, NigeriaSat-1, is sent into orbit on a Russian rocket.

2006

Nigeria cedes the oil-rich Bakassi Peninsula to Cameroon, following a ruling by the International Court of Justice. With revenues from sky-high oil prices Nigeria becomes the first African country to repay its debts to the Paris Club, the group representing the financial institutions of wealthy countries.

2007

The presidential election is won by Umaru Musa Yar'Adua, of the People's Democratic Party (the same party as

Obasanjo). His government has to deal with the fundamentalist group Boko Haram's insurrection, which is responsible for hundreds of deaths. The president dies in 2010 following a long illness, leaving his position to his vice-president, Goodluck Jonathan, who wins the election the following year.

2013

The government declares a state of emergency in three northern states and sends in the army to fight Boko Haram. In 2014 the terrorists kidnap nearly three hundred girls from a school in Chibok, Borno State, and launch a series of attacks, capturing a number of towns around Lake Chad, but are later pushed back by a military coalition of forces from Nigeria, Chad, Cameroon and Niger.

2015

Former general Muhammadu Buhari (who led the 1983 coup), having been defeated in 2007 and 2011, becomes the first opposition candidate in Nigerian history to win the presidential election. Low oil prices bring the country to the brink of a financial crisis. Over the following years thousands of people are displaced following clashes between herders and farmers in the states of Benue and Taraba, caused, in part, by the effects of climate change in the Sahel. Boko Haram targets army bases.

2019

Despite the health issues that force him to hand over the reins to his vice-president several times, Buhari is re-elected for a second term. In 2020 demonstrations break out against the police – more specifically, the Special Anti-Robbery Squad, or SARS – which is accused of torture and other crimes. The protests claim over sixty lives, and on at least one occasion the army opens fire on unarmed demonstrators.

2021

Buhari bans Twitter for over six months (earning the approval of Donald Trump) after the social media platform suspends his account over some incendiary declarations regarding the renewed Igbo separatist movement in the south-east of the country.

regional demands for the powerful federal government to devolve more economic and political power to the states.

Ignoring the new political environment and frequently using a military sledgehammer to suppress civil agitations has had severe consequences. After the return to democracy in 1999, the ignored reformist agitations of the military-rule era erupted violently. The political competition of democracy (which was absent under military rule) opened opportunities for disaffected groups to deploy violence as a means of addressing their grievances and gaining access to power and economic resources, which they felt had been denied them. After 1999 a plethora of armed ethnic or regional militias, vigilantes and insurgent groups rose up to challenge the state. Although each of these groups has different aims, all of them directed their hostility against the government.

As a result, even though Nigeria is now governed by an elected civilian government, the military has been preoccupied by security challenges with roots in the pre-democratic era.

These security challenges have led to a highly militarised society in which soldiers are dispersed in civilian spaces throughout the country. Although Nigeria's military ostensibly left government in 1999, its soldiers are currently engaged in the largest peacetime military deployment in its history. Soldiers are currently deployed in internal security operations in at least thirty-two of Nigeria's thirty-six states to fight the insurgents of Boko Haram, kidnappers, armed robbers and other outbursts of insecurity. A former chief of army staff, Lieutenant-General Abdulrahaman Bello Danbazau, said at the inaugural Freedom House Democracy Lecture Series in Lagos,

THE PASSENGER   Max Siollun

Opposite: A protester addresses an officer in front of the Nigeria Police Force headquarters during the #EndSARS protest in Abuja.
Page 37: An #EndSARS protester waves a miniature Nigerian flag.

'It is not normal ... in Nigeria today, the armed forces are the ones doing the duties of the police.' Although the Boko Haram insurgency is constantly in the headlines, two other rebellions deserve mention because of their potential to destabilise the country.

THE BLESSING AND CURSE OF OIL

Throughout Nigeria's existence, every government has grappled with two existential national problems: how to share political power, and make everyone feel included in a country with hundreds of different ethnic groups, and how to share the country's oil wealth. Both of these problems intersect in the oil industry.

Nigeria's wealth lies in the oilfields near its southern coastline (see 'The Niger Delta' on page 161). This crude-oil wealth is simultaneously a reason for the country's unity and a motivation for

THE POSTHUMOUS BENEFACTOR

For almost half of its post-colonial history Nigeria has been under a military dictatorship – from 1966 to 1999, with a brief democratic interlude between 1979 and 1983. In many respects the harshest military regime was the last, under General Sani Abacha, who took power in 1993 having been involved in *every single one* of the country's previous coups. A career soldier with various government roles on his résumé, he banned almost all political activity and surrounded himself with a 3,000-strong personal security force. At the same time as sending troops to restore democracy in Liberia and Sierra Leone, he repressed any dissent at home. His most brutal act was the death sentence and execution of the writer and environmental campaigner Ken Saro-Wiwa and other Ogoni activists in 1995, which resulted in Abacha being ostracised by the West. His sudden death in 1998 – officially of a heart attack, but there was also talk of poisoning – cleared the way for the transition to civilian rule, which has lasted to this day. After his death the general was accused of having stolen $5 billion from state coffers, putting him in fourth place, behind Suharto, Marcos and Mobutu, in a special league table of dictators who have enriched themselves at their country's expense. Following an agreement between his successor Olusegun Obasanjo's government and the Abacha family, and after a lengthy hunt for the funds hidden in bank accounts in various countries – which is still ongoing – most of the money has been returned to Nigeria in instalments, with the result that Abacha has been described, ironically, as a benevolent ancestor who, from the land of the dead, continues to donate generously to the governments that have succeeded him.

its disintegration. Oil exports generate approximately 90 per cent of the country's foreign exchange earnings. Nigeria's constitution vests ownership of crude oil in the federal government, which collects oil revenues and then divides it among all the states. However, 80 per cent of Nigeria's oil is obtained from only four of the country's states, all of them located in the deep south. Four states bearing the overwhelming financial burden for the remaining thirty-two makes conflict a near certainty. The oil-producing states became aggrieved that oil drilled from their land causes environmental devastation, polluting their farms, crops and rivers, yet is used to enrich other parts of Nigeria. Such grievances, coupled with massive youth unemployment in the oil-producing areas, erupted violently when youths armed themselves, formed militant groups and waged an insurgency from 2004 to protest about economic exploitation and environmental pollution. They sabotaged oil pipelines, attacked oil installations and kidnapped oil workers. The insurgency severely disrupted Nigeria's oil production and economy and led to an increase in global oil prices. It caused a near 50 per cent reduction in Nigeria's oil output and cost the country approximately $100 billion in lost oil revenue between 2003 and 2008.

In June 2009 the federal government ended the insurgency by convincing more than 25,000 militants to lay down their weapons in exchange for an amnesty and the government paying them a monthly cash salary. Although the amnesty programme ended the violence and allowed oil extraction to resume, it did not address its root causes and also set a dangerous 'cash-for-guns' precedent by giving the impression that violence pays.

THE GHOSTS OF BIAFRA

Nigeria's 'forgive-and-forget' attitude to national crises such as the oil insurgency and the civil war generated new, unintended crises. Since the government refused to release an official narrative of the civil war, few lessons were learned from it. The absence of official accounts led others to fill the void. Strangely, the civil war's history has largely been written by the war's losers rather than its winners. Since Igbos could not articulate their grievances through formal channels such as a war-crimes trial or a truth-and-reconciliation commission, they have produced a huge body of literature about the conflict. Barely a year goes by without an Igbo author publishing a book about it – one of the most successful African novels of the past two decades, *Half of a Yellow Sun* by Chimamanda Ngozi Adichie, is set during that period (see 'An Author Recommends' on page 186).

Although there was supposedly 'no victor, no vanquished', Igbos complain that, more than fifty years on, Nigeria does not view them as equal citizens. No Igbo has been president of Nigeria since the war ended, and Igbos are barely represented in senior government leadership positions. The constant Igbo discourse about the war generated two new trends in the 21st century: a feeling among many Igbos that Nigeria regards them as a fifth column and is still punishing them for the secession over half a century ago, and renewed agitation for another secession.

In order to share power between Nigeria's north and south, each of the two regions takes turns to produce the president. The incumbent, President Buhari, is from the north, and after he completes his second and final term of office in 2023, his successor should be a southerner. Returning power back to the south will

NATIONAL YOUTH SERVICE CORPS

In 1973, three years after the end of the Nigerian Civil War, in a country rocked by ethnic conflicts, the National Youth Service Corps (NYSC) was established. The aim of this compulsory government programme for new university and polytechnic graduates was to promote national unity. To this day 300,000 young people each year are sent to a different state from their own for an orientation period – three weeks of military-style training in camps subject to harsh discipline – followed by a year of work in sectors such as education, health or infrastructure. Those who do not complete the service risk a fine or imprisonment, even though the penalties are rarely applied. More to the point, without completion they would find it much more difficult to find work in the public sector as well as many private companies. It goes without saying that people from modest backgrounds cannot afford to miss out on it. Schools are the main destination for the young participants because of a lack of teaching staff, so pupils are entrusted to often poorly prepared teachers. NYSC members receive a monthly salary of 33,000 naira (around $75), but the real benefit is the ability to make connections, which are hugely important in a society like Nigeria, which is organised around personal relationships. Unfortunately, however, taking part in the programme is growing increasingly unsafe. New graduates are often sent to rural areas where it is dangerous to travel because of the presence of bandits or ethnic or religious violence. In the north-east of the country, the NYSC's distinctive white uniforms mark them out as targets for members of Boko Haram, representing the Western education that the terrorists are trying to purge from their territory.

solve one problem and create another. If a southerner other than a south-easterner succeeds Buhari, it would mean that the mainly Igbo south-east would be the only part of southern Nigeria that has not been given a chance to produce a president since the return to democracy almost twenty-five years ago, thus making Igbos feel even more alienated.

THE MILITARY AND HUMAN RIGHTS

Buhari's successor will also have to deal with the military problem. The broad and intense nature of Nigeria's security challenges means that military influence on daily life is unlikely to diminish in the near future. The military's wide deployment in society has generated friction with the civilian communities in which it operates and has led to accusations of widespread human-rights abuses.

The latter years of military rule in the late 1990s were characterised by a pro-democracy movement to end military rule and the increasingly repressive behaviour of military governments and security agencies, which arbitrarily arrested, tortured, murdered or exiled pro-democracy activists, human-rights campaigners, trade union leaders and other opponents of the government. These abuses went unpunished and created a culture of military superiority over, and contempt for, civilians. Civil-society groups complained that some soldiers still carry military-era attitudes in these democratic times, and examples of military human-rights abuses are legion.

In 1999 and 2001 soldiers invaded the communities of Odi, Bayelsa State, and Zaki-Biam, Benue State, respectively, using heavy weapons including artillery and mortar bombs and killing hundreds of unarmed civilians, razing houses in retaliation for the killing of security officers

Igbo separatism, which was subdued during the thirty years of military dictatorship that followed the Biafran War, re-emerged with the return to democracy, fuelled by a widespread feeling of marginalisation in the south-east of the country, the region where all the oilfields are concentrated and therefore the bulk of Nigeria's wealth. This is precisely why it would be almost impossible for the Nigerian government to accept an independent Biafra, while the situation simultaneously encourages the separatists to push for it – and tensions eventually exploded into open conflict in 2021. The first secessionist groups were non-violent, but the federal government's harsh repression helped to radicalise the movement, which since the 2010s has been reorganised under the banner of the Indigenous People of Biafra (IPOB), created by Nnamdi Kanu, the director of Radio Biafra in London. The station broadcasts incendiary speeches railing against the corrupt, ineffective and violent government in Abuja. Kanu was arrested in Lagos in 2015 but fled abroad after his release. In late 2020 he announced the creation of the military wing of IPOB, the Eastern Security Network, which was involved in various armed clashes with the army in 2021 and allied with other ethnically based groups in the Niger Delta that have been targeting the government and the oil companies with bombings, kidnappings and killings since the 1990s in their campaign for the redistribution of oil money. Arrested again in June 2021 by Interpol, Kanu was extradited to Nigeria – a heavy blow for the separatists – but Igboland remains a powder keg.

> '**A new leadership less beholden to military interests may be less conservative and more willing to embrace the tectonic reforms that military-led governments resisted.**'

in both communities. A serving army officer later admitted that 'by the time the soldiers left [Odi] only a church, a community centre and a bank were left standing … Everything else was destroyed.'

In March 2014 the army responded to an attempt by Boko Haram to free its inmates detained at a military barracks in north-east Nigeria by killing 600 of the detainees as they tried to escape. The Giwa Barracks incident caused such a rupture in relations between Nigeria and the USA that a former US State Department official described it to me as 'a nail in the coffin' of US military assistance to Nigeria. The USA consequently blocked Nigerian government requests to purchase American military equipment.

The civilian #EndSARS protests in 2021 against Nigeria's Special Anti-Robbery Squad (SARS), along with demands that the squad be disbanded, was probably the zenith of civilian discontent against abuses by security forces. However, Nigeria's government cannot give the civilian population what it wants by withdrawing soldiers from the streets without causing chaos. Nigeria is in a rock-and-a-hard-place dilemma. It can reduce civilian–military friction by withdrawing soldiers, but that would amplify the country's security problems by allowing insurgents to run amok in the military's absence.

LAST RIDE FOR THE CLASS OF 1966?
The 2023 presidential election will also be a watershed for other reasons. Over the last fifty-seven years, Nigeria has had only one president who had no personal or family involvement in the 1966 crisis and the ensuing civil war. Despite the military's long grip on political leadership, Buhari's presidency might be its last ride. The class of 1966 are now septuagenarian or octogenarian grandfathers or are deceased. In December 2021 Lieutenant-General Mohammed Wushishi (a millionaire businessman and retired civil-war veteran) died. President Buhari will be eighty when he leaves office, Obasanjo will be almost eighty-six and General Ibrahim Babangida (another former military ruler) will be eighty-one and is in poor health. Nigeria's next government is unlikely to be heavily linked to the military governments of the past.

For more than fifty years Nigeria's generals have successfully rejected opposition demands for national restructuring and the devolution of power to state governments. A new leadership less beholden to military interests might be less conservative and more willing to embrace the tectonic reforms that military-led governments resisted. If so, for the first time in several generations, Nigerian politicians will have to ride without military officers looking over their shoulders and stabilising that ride when it gets too bumpy. This is both an opportunity and a challenge. While it offers Nigerian politics a chance to make a clean break with its military past, what will the country be like without the experience of its retired-generals' club? 🖋

Welcome to Arewa: An Ocean in the Savannah

Take a trip to Nigeria's troubled but fascinating and influential north. This ancient land has navigated centuries of religious turmoil and is home to peoples who are at odds with one another in every way – despite which, they are united by a particular fatalism and a shared substrate of traditions, rules and ways of thinking.

ABUBAKAR ADAM IBRAHIM

A young boy shows off his horse during the Durbar festival in Zaria, Kaduna State.

T he place most northerners call home is a vast expense of open land that sprawls between the Sahara Desert to the north and the rainforest belt to the south that cuts it off from the southern tribes and from the coast where the restless Atlantic laps the shores. Yet, stranded between these two extremes, in character this region is more like the ocean – old, immense, beautiful, sometimes calm, sometimes turbulent and strangely, seductively mysterious. Most people who live here call it Arewa, the Hausa word for 'north'.

When this region is mentioned in news aimed at an international audience, it is on account of Boko Haram, the terror group, whose abduction of some three hundred schoolgirls in April 2014 put them on a global map and caused international celebrities, including Michelle Obama, to trend the hashtag #BringBackOurGirls. Either that or the kidnappings for ransom by gunmen lurking in the region's vast forests of stunted trees and thorny shrubs. These bandits have mastered the art of abduction, from a handful of travellers on the roads, or targeting people in their homes, or sometimes herding six hundred schoolboys from their hostel at gunpoint into their forest strongholds.

But those who know this region, like the fishes know the ocean deep, those who call it Arewa, will tell you that it has its charms.

Sometimes, it feels as if swathes of the north are like a street circus. On weekly market days, traders in shea butter, milkmaids, herdsmen and artisans bundle their wares off to the marketplace. Hyenas, snakes, crocodiles and monkeys go, too, led by street performers.

The hyenas, strapped in muzzles woven from sisal, run at the roaring audience, only held back by the leashes their masters hold. These men are often dressed in dashikis with a range of amulets and charms strapped across their biceps, necks and waists. Their tasselled tutus of strands of crimson, neon-green and yellow threads sway as they move while dancing or wrestling the animals. The secret of hyena whispering, croc cradling and snake charming is often passed down from generation to generation. And besides entertainment and a dramatic adrenaline rush, the performers often provide another service, as medicine men. From alternative antivenin for snake bite to herbal remedies for aches, ulcers, pneumonia or colds. Some even offer a cure for cancer. Bedwetting children, wailing

ABUBAKAR ADAM IBRAHIM is a writer and journalist originally from Jos and now living in Abuja. His short stories and other works have received numerous awards, including the BBC African Performance Prize for his play *A Bull Man's Story*, while his report on Boko Haram, published by Granta in 2017, won the Michael Elliott Award for Excellence in African Storytelling. His debut novel, *Season of Crimson Blossoms* (Cassava Republic, 2017), which has been translated into French, German and Tamil, won the Nigeria Prize for Literature 2018. His latest novel is *When We Were Fireflies* (2023).

and kicking, are mounted on the hyenas. If the fright alone doesn't keep the children awake at night and stop them from wetting the bed, the small parcels of herbal powder handed to the parents to be mixed into the children's food or drink should do the trick. They don't always.

While the hyena men could claim descent from the *sarkin dawa* (the lord of the wilds), the croc men often claim their lineage from the *sarkin ruwa* (the river lord), whose mastery of rivers and their mysteries gives them dominion over creatures of the deep and helps them cure pain and fevers. Often they sell medicines for improved sexual prowess. They are not ashamed of it. Neither are the people who patronise them. The trade in aphrodisiacs in the north is very old. Not even the region's vaunted cultural values of modesty and censorship or the religious revival – which started in the late 1970s, blossomed in the 1990s and continues to burn fervently today – have been able to slow it down.

At the Friday mosques or the markets in every town, the voices of the aphrodisiac merchants blare through public-address systems mounted on cars or push-carts, advertising, in colourful language, the efficacy of their drugs, mocking the failed or failing virility of their potential customers and emphasising that marital sex, and proficiency in its performance, is a fundamental service to God. It is all a strange mix. But it is a message that has carried.

For a region thought to be sexually frugal, it is ironic that the best aphrodisiacs are traded here from under the veil and very much out in the open.

The female variant is called *kayan mata*, which, in Hausa, means 'women's stuff' or 'women's things'. It has become a profitable business that has put millions in some sex merchants' bank accounts. In

WOMEN'S THINGS

Like stimulating products for men, *kayan mata*, literally 'women's things' – recipes for aphrodisiacs consisting of herbs, roots, seeds and fruits – have existed for centuries, passed down from women to girls as a means of preparing young brides for their wedding night or of guaranteeing their husband's favours in a society, the north, where polygamy is legal and common. What has changed in recent years is the advent of Instagram and other social media, which have opened up what has traditionally been an invisible market (and one reserved only for married women) to entrepreneurship and marketing. While *kayan mata* were once associated with juju – love potions and spells used by women to bewitch their husbands or steal men away from their legitimate wives (a plot device regularly found in Nollywood films) – the sellers' messaging now focuses on natural ingredients and pleasure. Good sex rather than magic will ensure a husband's fidelity. The success of these new entrepreneurs, who offer home delivery and customer care, has provided the north with a rare export to the south. And on Instagram it has created a space in which to talk more openly about sexuality, including such taboos as the female orgasm. That said, gossip is what draws people to social media: for the 1.3 million followers of Jaruma (@jaruma_empire) – the sex therapist 'to the stars', who sells tonics such as Divorce Is Not My Portion (for 500,000 naira, around $1,125), Love Me Like Crazy (250,000 naira) and Ecstacy 9 (65,000 naira) – the attraction lies in her famous clients, from generals who fail to pay their bills to celebrity marriages consummated thanks to her products.

shops, market stalls and on social media, the products are displayed in jars, vials and packs. Based on the open display, the sheer volume of trade, it is safe to say there is good business going on in the bedrooms in this part of the country. That may explain the region's booming population, which will help propel Nigeria to the 400-million mark in 2050, overtaking the USA.

SMALL GODS ON A SMALL HILL

Once upon a time the plateau on top of Dala Hill in Kano was home to the gods of the Hausa people. They were humanoid supernaturals – wily spirit beings who granted favours, misfortune and curses in return for sacrifices, sometimes of blood or small animals, sometimes bigger ones and even humans. At other times their requests were for less gory things: food, drink and some zany acts in a form of worship that came to be known as Bori, the Hausa animist faith of the ancients. These spirits, gods or imps were not content on the Dala. They would possess humans, prompting a wild exorcism of dancing and self-flagellation. When the Muslims came they gave these spirit beings another name, djinns, and in the 14th century replaced the animist religion with Islam.

Little remains of the tangible and intangible heritage of this past. In Kano's famous Gidan Makama Museum only a small vestibule is dedicated to the pre-Islamic heritage of the Hausa people. Even the name of the most famous Hausa god of the time, Tsumburburra, is now lost to many. In the late 1980s and 1990s Bori adherents still wandered the streets,

offering spiritual services to those who needed them. Today their ceremonies are confined to the fringes of society. Unseen. Unheard. Except by a few.

Religion is fundamental to the northerners. It always has been. From the moment Dala the blacksmith settled on the hill that would later bear his name and organised spirit worship for the society that gathered at his feet – a task perfected by the most famous pre-Islamic religious figure, Barbushe – religion has been central to community building in the north. The community that sprang from the hill has always tied state and religion. Ever since that time the core of the north has been woven from the strands of different faiths. Today the friction between these strands has continued to strum the chord of discord in the region.

The brushstrokes of Islam brought a whole new colour to the tapestry, a colour that soaked and absorbed as much of the region as it could, spreading from Maiduguri, where the Kanuris on the fringes of the Sahara had long embraced the faith, to Kano, once the pagan capital, all the way to Sokoto to the north-west, which would, during the 19th century, become the capital of a vast Islamic empire.

Before that occurred, for four hundred years the azan call of Islam and the ancient chants of the animists rang out side by side. At the beginning of the 19th century a Fulani revivalist, Shehu Usman Dan Fodio, who, oppressed by the Hausa king of Gobir, migrated with his followers, regrouped and decided to launch a holy war against

'For four hundred years the azan call of Islam and the ancient chants of the animists rang out side by side.'

Two sisters, both of whom were
kidnapped by Boko Haram terrorists on
separate occasions in 2015, pose for a
portrait at a camp for internally displaced
people in Maiduguri, Borno State.

the Hausa kings, who comfortably mixed Islam with pagan practices. By 1803 Dan Fodio had deposed the Hausa rulers, replacing them with Fulani emirs and establishing a caliphate, a holy Muslim empire, that stretched into parts of what are now northern Cameroon, southern Niger, most of the north of Nigeria and the fringes of Burkina Faso. But the southerly expansion of his empire was resisted by a coalition of the pagan tribes of the plains and hills and the nagging tsetse flies that infected his cavalry with sleeping sickness. A century later these same tribes eagerly embraced the Christian missionaries who brought clothes and Bibles and offered them protection from the slave raids of the mounted Muslims. When British colonial forces toppled the caliphate and killed Sultan Attahiru in battle in 1902, it was easy for the pagan minorities to see that a saviour had come.

This history – of conquests and failed domination, slave raids, broken gods and imported faiths – is at the heart of the violence singeing the north of Nigeria today.

REKINDLED CANDLES ON OLD ALTARS
Of all the cities in the north, perhaps Jos is the one most appealing to foreigners. It prided – and this use of the past tense is deliberate – itself and advertised itself as the home of 'peace and tourism'. Yes, it has amazing rock formations to see, it has some great waterfalls, a zoo and a wildlife reserve and perhaps the most pleasant weather in the country.

In 2001 Muslims and Christians, who had lived here together for nearly a century, left their businesses, ran to their homes and fetched shovels, diggers, pitchforks, clubs and guns and went to war against each other. It was the most inexplicable descent into mass hysteria, one that had roots in the centuries-old history of religious strife mentioned above.

The mostly Christian indigenous groups, who gloated about their fathers' resistance to the jihadi forces of old, had accepted Jesus, and the Muslims, who after a century had circled back to the revivalist teachings of Dan Fodio, clashed. The immediate cause was some inconsequential appointment of a Muslim man to a position the Christians felt they were entitled to. Hundreds died, thousands of houses were torched and the innocence for which the city was famed was forever lost.

However, it was not the first major religious riot in the region that had fatal consequences. Since the 1970s nomads, who are mostly Fulani and Muslim, have increasingly clashed with farmers, who are sometimes local Hausa Muslims and at other times Christian minorities. When these clashes take place with Christians, the religious angle is played up. The herdsmen's intransigence is interpreted as a continuation of Dan Fodio's jihad. The defence of the homeland is often interpreted as a religious duty – after all, state and faith are often intertwined in these parts. Grand interpretations are introduced, conspiracy theories are spun and more fuel is tossed into the flame. And, like a ripple on a pond, the ramifications travel far and wide across the great seascape of the region and the country.

In truth, it is often simply a case of some inconsiderate nomad just wanting to feed his herd and deciding the lush farm he saw would provide good fodder for his animals. Global warming and increasing insecurity in the northern extremities, no thanks to cattle rustlers, have pushed the nomads further south to find pasture for their herds, bringing them into conflict with the farming populations closer to and within the forest regions to the south. Over time the intensity and frequency of these conflicts have increased.

It is impossible to blame these clashes entirely on religion, yet it is impossible to remove religion from the mix.

By the 1970s the fading glow of post-independence promise that followed the end of British colonial rule in 1960 had descended into a sense of despair and

The story of Babban Gona reads like a fairy tale. A husband-and-wife team of Nigerian executives, graduates from top American universities, return to their home country, which is wracked by violent insurrections, and start to think about how to best to be of service. Studying the data on youth unemployment – a major reservoir for all criminal activity – and the Nigerian economy, they reach the conclusion that the sector with the greatest potential impact is agriculture. Eighty per cent of the food produced in sub-Saharan Africa comes from small farms, mainly family run, with around two hectares of land; at the same time, 70 per cent of the continent's poor are farmers. In Nigeria they earn on average $2 a day, and their productivity is exceptionally low. This was where Kola and Lola Masha identified a space to intervene. Inspired by the model of American cooperatives, they launched an agricultural revolution starting in the north: they offered credit to small farmers (on average $500 a year), empowered them by asking them to come together in 'trust groups' of three or four people (including a leader identified by Babban Gona) and trained them in how to improve their harvests, which the farmers were able to exploit fully without wastage thanks to the storage facilities provided by Babban Gona. More than 100,000 farmers have joined the programme, a quarter of them becoming shareholders, while the project continues to attract resources from private and public investment funds, from the Gates Foundation to the World Bank, offering them not just social investment but also a profitable business model, albeit one with narrow margins.

Number of violent deaths by state, 2011–21

The Nigeria Security Tracker, a Council on Foreign Relations project, has documented and mapped violence in Nigeria since 2011 (two years after a clash between the army and the terrorist group Boko Haram, which is often regarded as the beginning of the conflict between the Nigerian state and the terrorist group). Besides Boko Haram, which is active in the north, particularly in Borno State, various groups, starting with the army itself, are involved in violence that has led to an extremely high death toll. There are clashes between ethnic groups, between herders and farmers, new separatist movements – chiefly in the Niger Delta – and the police are also known to have undertaken extra-judicial killings.

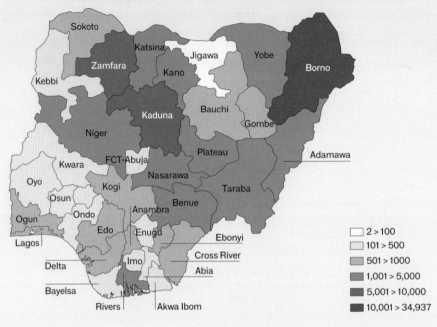

- 2 > 100
- 101 > 500
- 501 > 1000
- 1,001 > 5,000
- 5,001 > 10,000
- 10,001 > 34,937

Percentage of people beneath the poverty line by state, 2018–19

In the latest survey carried out by the National Bureau of Statistics, in 2018–19, the poverty line was calculated at 137,430 naira per annum (c. $310); 40 per cent of Nigerians live below this line.

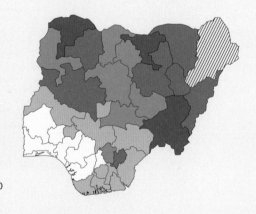

Percentage of the population
- 1–20
- 21–40
- 41–60
- 61–80
- 81–100
- N/A

SOURCE: NIGERIA SECURITY TRACKER, NBS – 2018/19 NIGERIAN LIVING STANDARDS SURVEY

Incidence of female genital mutilation (FGM) in women aged 15–49 by state, 2018

Across the country, 20 per cent of women aged between 15 and 49 have undergone FGM, down from 25 per cent in 2013. The prevalence is highest among Yoruba women (35 per cent), which helps to explain the higher incidence in the south-west. Among the main ethnic groups, only the Fulani do not practise FGM. All types of mutilation have been banned at a federal level since 2015, but only three states – Anambra, Ekiti and Oyo – have adopted the law.

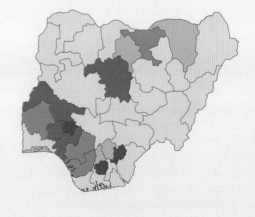

- 0–12%
- 13–26%
- 27–37%
- 38–50%
- 51–62%

Percentage of women aged 15–49 educated to at least secondary level by state, 2018

The percentage of women aged between 15 and 49 without any education has fallen since 2003, from 42 per cent to 35 per cent (for men, the figure is 22 per cent). The average number of school years completed rose from 5 to 6.5 over the same period, and 11 per cent of women and 17 per cent of men have been educated beyond secondary level.

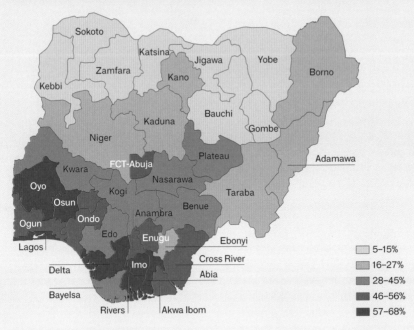

- 5–15%
- 16–27%
- 28–45%
- 46–56%
- 57–68%

SOURCE: 2018 DEMOGRAPHIC AND HEALTH SURVEY (DHS)

loss. The country wasn't working as well as everyone thought it would. A violent military coup had wiped out a crop of the post-independence leaders of the country, breaking irreparably any hope of a nation of diverse peoples, tribes and religions becoming a true collective.

With hope in men and their promises failing, people turned to God. A religious revival was triggered. A Sunni (Salafist) revival with roots in Dan Fodio's teachings arose to challenge the predominant and more laid-back Sufi orders. Pentecostal Christianity flourished and offered hope and shelter from the political and economic uncertainties and shunted aside the Catholic restraints of old. Rapid proselytisation began in both faiths, which provided a channel for the repressed fervour the people nursed. Islamic revivalism offered a return to the puritanism of Dan Fodio's preaching, and a return to Daulatul Islamiyya, an Islamic empire in which sharia rule applies, was touted as the way out. Champions of this alternative system drew many followers who were disenchanted by the prevalent corruption and the sustained failure of the Nigerian dream.

The new faith leaders milked the faithful of their meagre resources, grew fat and, like a plague, multiplied, splitting like cells and growing.

In a political climate a large following is a political asset. And, soon enough, politicians courted priests and a dangerous marriage began – or, perhaps more accurately, picked up where historical antecedents left off. Sometimes the implications of these unions are dire. Like the time certain politicians courted the outlier preacher Mohammed Yusuf in Maiduguri because of his popularity and large following. It emboldened his group of zealots, who wanted to take over the state and impose a tyranny of faith. The

They prefer contemplation to action, introspection to extroversion, spiritual to legal development, and as a result are seen as the mystics of Islam. Sufis, who belong almost exclusively to the Sunni tradition, are organised into orders or brotherhoods; in Nigeria there are two, the Qadiriyya and the Tijaniyyah, which are often in conflict. The former takes its name from the teacher Abdul-Qadir Gilani, who was active in Baghdad in the 12th century, and it is the oldest and most widespread Sufi order in the world, while the latter was founded in 1784 by Ahmad ibn Muhammad al-Tijani in Algeria. Both enjoy a high degree of legitimacy in Nigeria and operate a broad network of religious and social programmes that are important in keeping the fundamentalists at bay. In the eyes of the Salafis, who are wedded to a literal interpretation of the Qur'an, Sufism, with its emphasis on innovation and its veneration of saints, is a heretical movement to be fought in the same way as the infidels. In 2016, for example, a member of the Tijaniyyah was condemned to death for saying that the teacher Ibrahim Niasse was a greater figure than Muhammad. Since 2021 the order has been led by Muhammad Sanusi II, a prominent figure, and not only in the religious domain. Between 2009 and 2014 he was governor of the Central Bank of Nigeria and was also the whistleblower at the centre of a scandal that resulted in him losing his job when, in 2014, he wrote a letter to then President Goodluck Jonathan revealing the disappearance of $20 billion from the oil industry.

fallout between the two gave rise to what is today known as Boko Haram, the terror group that has for years successfully run a campaign of insurgency, killing thousands, closing down schools and crippling the fragile economy of the region.

TYRANTS AND POWER PLAY
In 1999 the decades of military dictatorships ended abruptly when the last tyrant, General Sani Abacha, a man from the north, keeled over and died at the height of his power. His death, with no designated successor, was so unexpected that there was uncertainty within the military as to how to proceed. Abacha's number two was at the time languishing in jail, accused of plotting a coup against his boss, so the military chose another general, Abdulsalam Abubakar, whose discharge letter from the army was on Abacha's desk waiting to be signed at the time of his death. Over the course of nine months Abdulsalam pushed the country through a transition process that ended with Olusegun Obasanjo, a retired general, a southerner and Christian from the Yoruba group, becoming president.

The north is far bigger than the other regions of Nigeria, and it clearly has the numbers to swing any election. It has a history of delivering block votes to whatever candidate it favours. Obasanjo was a beneficiary of this. Backed by the north, he won even when his own region, the south-west, voted against him. But in the north religion is always central to every discourse – even politics – and the northern elite's decision to back Obasanjo irked some people.

Under Obasanjo, a people and their frustrations, long shackled by military rule, were unleashed, and liberties unheard of during the dictatorships were pushed. Violent ethnic vigilantes arose in the Igbo-speaking south-east, and the Yoruba-speaking south-west had the Odua People's Congress, a feisty, pan-Yoruba group that basked in the glory of a Yoruba being president.

The north turned to religion for solace and distraction. Under the new freedoms allowed by the constitution, some states in the region adopted sharia – prescribed by Islam for judicial administration – for criminal law. It was a move that triggered both mass euphoria and hysteria in the region. While Muslims were wildly excited about it – save for a discerning few who saw it merely as a gimmick by the new political class to gain acceptance in the region – Christian minorities were deeply unsettled by a move they imagined would subjugate them and bring them under the folds of another religion.

They kicked. The Muslims kicked back, and soon the two were at each other's throats like squabbling children – except in this instance there was blood. Hundreds were killed in violent religious and ethnic riots that scarred the face of the region. In cities such as Jos and Kaduna, the scars are so severe that exclusive Christian and exclusive Muslim districts sprang up, and a great geographical realignment took place. Over time the scars have healed – to some extent, at least – and visitors might not see them, but those who know will tell you that as a person of one faith, venturing into certain parts of town means entering into the open jaws of a shark. Because of the delicate balance, spontaneous riots could mean finding oneself at the mercy of an angry mob.

But to assume that the violence was exclusively religious or exclusively interfaith would be a mistake. These things are far more complicated.

*

THE PASSENGER   Abubakar Adam Ibrahim

Once upon a time in Lafia, capital of the North Central state of Nasarawa, a Sufi Muslim returning from a Mawlid feast celebrating the birth of Muhammad, the prophet of Islam (PBUH), was walking gingerly down the street, arms swinging, massive beads of his tasbih clicking as he went along. His flowing robe was emblazoned with the face of Sheikh Ibrahim Niasse, the most prominent Sufi figure in West Africa. A visiting Salafi Muslim took one look at him and called him a *mushrik* (a deviant Muslim). The Sufi responded with a blow. When questioned as to why he was attacking a visitor to the town, he proclaimed that the man had insulted the holiest figures in the faith, and those who had come to break up the fight between the two were so disgusted that they punched, kicked and spat at the Salafi, despite his protests that his words were misrepresented.

There is no love lost between the different groups of northern Nigeria's Muslims. The Salafis, who have grown exponentially over the last five decades, are always bickering with the Sufis, who themselves are bickering with the Shi'ites, who in their turn bicker with everyone else, including the government. Even the Salafis are split in two, and for years each faction has been vociferously opposed to the other. When the Christians are not in a quarrelsome engagement with their Muslim neighbours, the Catholics and the Pentecostals – the so-called prosperity churches – are constantly at each other's throats.

The local ruler's bodyguards pose for a portrait in a village in Taraba State.

But in 2002 a young firebrand Muslim preacher, Mohammed Yusuf, had risen in Maiduguri, capital of Borno state on the fringes of the Sahara. His repudiation of the Christian president and his rejection of the secular society into which Nigeria was being moulded brought him followers. His popularity made him 'eye candy' for politicians seeking popular support, and soon Yusuf, radical views and all, found himself in a position to greatly influence the governance of the state.

But his resentment towards a government that is not based on his strict interpretations of the Qur'an – which included denouncing Western education – soon led his supporters to clash with the security forces. The clashes escalated. Yusuf was killed, and his supporters scurried underground. They re-emerged as a group of guerrilla fighters, Boko Haram, which the world soon heard about. Yes, they have killed a lot of Christians, but they have killed many more Muslims for not sharing their ideology.

A SPECTACLE FOR THE SEASON

Every Eid al-Fitr, the Muslim holy feast that marks the end of Ramadan, or Eid al-Adha, the feast of the sacrifice, the most spectacular event in Nigeria plays out. Thousands of horses, bedecked in finery, are ridden out with their riders and attendants dressed in the most glamourous costumes – richly embroidered flowing robes, colourful turbans and fancy Moorish shoes, their upward-curving toes sometimes adorned with pom-poms. Every year thousands of tourists flock north to Kano, to Zaria and other old caliphate capitals to witness this grand display of elegance, power and an uncommon show of allegiance to the emir in spectacular events known as 'the Durbar'. Sometimes when a dignitary visits, a durbar is staged

for their entertainment – but these visitors have to be worth the trouble, because a durbar is never a small affair. Horses and their riders march in unison, charge and pull up just before the monarch, who is on a dais surrounded by his honoured guests, and wave their spears and swords in salute. Group after group, all dressed in the chosen livery of the houses or aristocrats they serve. All so elegant. Often different aristocratic houses or title holders organise a durbar group to charge and pledge loyalty to the monarch.

On the sidelines, hundreds gather, most of them in their Eid finery, to watch the spectacle. There are sideshows, and the street circuses have a field day, coaxing crowd-pleasing performances from their hyenas, monkeys, snakes and other performing animals. Vendors hawk their wares – ice cream, nuts, food-to-go wrapped in newspapers and handed out. Beyond the spectacle and the funfair, this is a fascinating display of the essence of the north. A devotion to faith and power. Years after colonisation, the deeply rooted

Some of the emir's guards taking part in the Durbar festival in Kaduna State.

feudal traditions have survived. The powerful elites have always held sway over the masses; the masses have mostly felt the need to remain subservient. This is deep in the foundation of the society, because the marriage of faith and religion at the heart of this culture confers a certain proximity to divinity on the rulers.

This delicate system – a culture, if you like – has built the north. It has also held it back. The system made it easy for the British, when they invaded in 1902, to set up a system of indirect rule where they conquered the emirs, installed new ones from the ruling houses and governed the region by proxy through them. The people always followed the guidance of their leaders.

In recent times this has translated into political power, and the north is perhaps the most powerful political bloc in the country. The size of the region's population and its tendency, by and large, to vote in the same way has ensured this. At first it was the leaders of the region telling the people who to vote for; now it is often faith leaders and sometimes the rote memory of a deeply entrenched and longstanding system that guides the region's political choices.

It has not always paid off, though. Yes, the north often backs the winning dog in the race – except in 2015 when Goodluck Jonathan (a southerner who, as vice-president, took the place of his deceased boss, President Umaru Musa Yar'Adua, a northerner) defied the odds to become president in his own right – but the region has remained one of the poorest in the country. The three states with the highest numbers of poor people are Sokoto, Taraba and Jigawa, all in the north, where no fewer than 87 per cent of the population live below the poverty line. This is according to data from the National

Bureau of Statistics. In keeping with the deviant spirit of irony that prevails in the region, the richest Black man in the world, Aliko Dangote, also happens to come from this same north.

The region's reputation for being poor has persisted and has often been used by the other regions to gloat at it, much to the irritation of northerners. Not many people complain about this poverty, however – in fact, there is a deeply felt sense of contentment, inspired by the fatalistic demands of faith. But in 2020 the gloating on social media provoked a reaction. A hashtag, #Arewatwitter, trended accompanying posts in which young northerners celebrating Eid posted pictures of their lavish lifestyles and their affluence, often posing in private jets, standing by Rolls-Royces, Maseratis, G-Wagons and BMWs. For many on social media, whose limited knowledge of the region meant only the association with poverty, it was a humbling lesson that, while the north might at first glance appear to be extremely poor, it is actually also filthy rich.

CHILDREN OF THE WINDS AND SANDS
For a visitor driving or walking down the streets of Yola, the alleyways of Minna or the pathways in a small village in Kogi State by the River Niger, it is not uncommon to find children with unwashed faces in worn, ripped clothes wandering the streets, bowls in hands. Their songs are poignant, tugging at the heartstrings, asking for food or some change.

This indomitable army of the *almajirai* – children entrusted to the care of Islamic scholars to memorise the Qur'an – is everywhere. They travel with their teachers across the region, far from their homes and their parents, whom they don't see for

ALIKO DANGOTE

A devout Muslim of Hausa ethnicity with a net worth estimated at almost $14 billion, Aliko Dangote, the 'Prince of Kano', his native city, is the richest man in Africa. Having lost his father – a wealthy peanut exporter – at the age of eleven, Aliko was raised by his maternal grandfather, Sanusi Dantata, the heir to an influential trading family and former director of the Shell-BP consortium in Nigeria. Dangote is received everywhere like a head of state, and his empire is the continent's largest private employer, present in eighteen African countries, even though its core business is in his native Nigeria, where he enjoys political support that has enabled him to gain a foothold in a number of key sectors subject to privatisation. Furthermore, 'it is no coincidence that many products on Nigeria's import ban lists are items in which Dangote has major interests', according to remarks made by an American diplomat intercepted by WikiLeaks in 2007. This has led to a monopoly situation, particularly in the cement industry, in which he controls 70 per cent of the domestic market, and in sugar, in which he leads the field in Africa. His group is also active in telecommunications, property, banking, sport and food, but the definitive breakthrough came with his venture into oil. The construction of a mega-refinery in the Lekki Free Zone near Lagos promises to solve the paradox of the country being dependent on foreign countries for refined products in spite of its abundant reserves of black gold. As a philanthropist, he works on humanitarian projects with the foundations established by Bill and Melinda Gates and Bono. His lifelong dream, however, is in a different league: to buy his beloved Arsenal Football Club.

Two friends playing during the Eid al-Adha
celebrations in Zaria, Kaduna State.

Welcome to Arewa: An Ocean in the Savannah

> '**The mix of poverty, illiteracy and a blooming, vibrant population means there is a naive army waiting to be recruited by zealots and desperate politicians.**'

years at a time. UNICEF reports that there are about ten million such children on the streets, which constitutes about 81 per cent of the thirteen million out-of-school children in the country. All these *almajirai* are from the north.

It is a system that is very old. The name *almajiri* (singular) is from the Arabic word *almuhajir*, meaning one who migrates, either in search of knowledge or religious freedom. The federal government has debated how to get these children off the streets but lacks the commitment to go against the old religious order, which claims the practice is a fundamental way of life for them. Not all these children become the religious scholars their parents hoped they would. Many cannot cope with the rigours of begging and the brutal teaching sessions, conducted under the supervision of a whip-bearing teacher. Most of them do not acquire any formal education or life skills. When political riots break out, fingers are often pointed in their direction. They are considered free-range thugs-for-hire. However, that is not always the case, and while some become problematic, many develop into responsible, if damaged, members of the community.

Abubakar Shekau, the infamous Boko Haram leader, once declared the most wanted man in Nigeria with the USA placing a $7 million bounty on his head, was a product of this system. His parents surrendered him to the care of an itinerant teacher with whom he travelled around until he settled in Maiduguri

and eventually became a follower of Mohammed Yusuf. He had seen his mother only a few times after, and in two separate interviews, for the Voice of America and in the Nigerian newspaper the *Daily Trust*, she confessed there was little in the way of a relationship between her and her son.

Boko Haram, which Shekau headed until he was killed in May 2021 following infighting within the group, did not suddenly appear out of a vacuum. Mohammed Yusuf's preaching resonated in an echo chamber of an old culture and system that is still struggling to adapt to the realities of the modern world. The north has always looked at Western education with suspicion. They had Islam and a system of knowledge long before the British came and murdered their leaders. For the average northerner, state and religion have always been one and the same. Once colonialism was entrenched, many northerners refused to send their children to school, fearing the erasure of their faith or the corruption of their morals. The anti-school propaganda was phenomenally successful, such that over a hundred years later countless parents still have doubts about sending children to school. It has proven costly to the region.

Since independence in 1960 the north has been playing catch-up. Post-independence leaders of the region, like Sardauna Sir Ahmadu Bello, the first premier of the old political division of Northern Nigeria, realised that if the north were to develop it would have to achieve parity with the other regions in terms of education. A rash of schools and institutions were built, parents were encouraged to enrol children in them and those who had had rudimentary education were encouraged to pursue further studies. That mad dash to catch up was truncated when these leaders were assassinated in the bloody coup of 1966.

Literacy levels in the region have remained phenomenally low, which has been a problem in many ways. The mix of poverty, illiteracy and a blooming, vibrant population means there is a naive army waiting to be recruited by zealots and desperate politicians. With the idea that state and religion are one already deep-rooted in the culture, it is easy for young people to be lured by the idea of somehow rekindling a utopian vision. It has worked for the worse in many ways, with different spiritual leaders, such as Maitatsine in the 20th century and later Mohammed Yusuf, easily raising armies of havoc-wreakers. In the hands of a 'mad Titan' like Shekau, with a global terror network to draw on, this iteration of this army has proven deadly, competent and quite adept at performing inhuman acts and dismembering a tottering country.

To add to the menace, in the north-west dangerous groups of gunmen, mostly former nomads with an intimate knowledge of the region's forests, have perfected the art of kidnapping hundreds of school-children and travellers and massacring villagers. In January 2022 they killed about two hundred villagers in Zamfara as a reprisal for a military raid that left about a hundred bandits dead. These gangs, travelling on motorcycles through the forest terrain, rifles slung over their shoulders, are so endemic that they have imposed levies on some villagers. Pay to access your farms or be killed. With little help coming from the government, most villagers pay. In some cases that has not been enough to save them. Thousands have had to flee their villages to the regional capitals, abandoning their homes and their farms.

In one attack, in December 2021, these bandits abducted more than six hundred students from a school in Katsina. Many schools have been forced to close. Many parents are afraid to send their children to school. What little gains had been made in educating the population have suffered a huge setback. It will take years to recover. It will take even longer to catch up.

These bandits are mostly Fulani, nomads who have lost their cattle to other criminals and have turned to crime as a way of surviving. It pays them. Billions of naira have been handed over in ransoms for the return of kidnapped relatives. And, like the orcas of the deep sea, these bands of criminals have defied the Nigerian government and its security forces, small in number, badly equipped, badly motivated and spread too thinly across all the flashpoints in the country. These flash-points are as numerous as eyes in the seas.

DEEP, DEEP BLUE SAND

When most people from elsewhere cast a cursory glance across the vast expanse of the Sahel belt in which the north sits, they see a blank uniform space, a void that like a mindless creature moves in unison, thumbprint-votes en masse in elections, often making bad political choices on behalf of the rest of the country.

But the region is far more than that. There might be a prevailing culture, a common identity of sorts, a common lingua franca – Hausa – spoken across the region and in neighbouring countries, but there are hundreds of ethnic minorities and languages here, some of them with as few as a thousand speakers, all of

Left: A young farmer tends to his crops in his greenhouse in Jos, Plateau State.
Below: Farmers returning from their land in Gembu, Taraba State.

them with their own unique identity and culture. These identities may be subsumed into the general body of what is often portrayed in the film industry known as Kannywood. The name is derived, of course, from Hollywood, but since the heart of this film industry is centred on Kano, they tinkered and created something that should be original. Except it isn't, much like the movies the filmmakers produce – and they produce a lot of them.

The movies are mostly domestic dramas, about love and deceit. In the early days they were mostly super-low-budget pastiches of Bollywood movies, sometimes with the storyline ripped off wholesale and adapted to its new location. While over time they have increasingly looked within their own culture for their stories, the dancing and music, often characterised by excessive use of AutoTune, have remained. But these films have become a huge cultural phenomenon, providing a livelihood for thousands and entertainment – and sometimes an escape – for millions.

Smaller, divergent groups in the region have taken their cue from the huge industry and turned their lens inwards. They are now producing films in local languages and are taking greater pride in the music they produce. Like Kannywood, they, too, are pastiching the name, one example being Igawood, produced by Igala-speaking people on the banks of the Niger further south.

Despite the horrors perpetrated in the region's hinterlands, people in the north behave as if all is calm, often displaying a baffling lack of outrage over the calamities. Understanding the north means understanding the overall philosophy that guides life there, which often derives from religion. The most prevalent is the concept of *qaddara*, or fate. The northerner believes deeply that nothing ever happens without the sanction of God. If bad things happen, it is as God wills it; the same when good things happen. For others this may seem incredibly hard to accept, but a typical northerner is raised not to argue with fate, and this attitude has kept the region seemingly calm about the situation. It is the reason why farmers sometimes defy bandits and march to their farms. If they are fated to perish, they cannot escape that fate. It is also why they accept government failings with such sobriety. Because, in the end, the best justice is not that of man but that which God will dispense. The bond between a northerner and their faith, be they Christian or Muslim, is often overwhelming. It is something that helps them cope. It is why religion is probably the only thing they will fight for.

So, far from the troubles or shortly after them, at the markets cars honk their horns, blasting out AutoTune soundtracks from Kannywood movies, drowning out the melancholy chants of the *almajirai*, competing with the blaring voice of the aphrodisiac seller over a public-address system, the clank-clank of the rickety taxi making way for the roar of a Maserati zapping by, the muezzin calling the faithful to prayer and the happy, zesty worship songs from the church in the corner.

Welcome to Arewa. 🐦

STILL
BECOMING

CHIMAMANDA NGOZI ADICHIE

Buses near the Obalende Bus Terminus
in Lagos.

Lagos makes no attempt to welcome you or earn your love, and yet Nigeria's most populous city continues to draw in an ever-expanding population from all over the country and right across the African continent. Nigerian literary icon Chimamanda Ngozi Adichie introduces us to the city's paradoxes and continual transformations.

63

Lagos will not court you. It is a city that is what it is. I have lived part-time in Lagos for ten years and I complain about it each time I return from my home in the US – its allergy to order, its stultifying traffic, its power cuts. I like, though, that nothing about Lagos was crafted for the tourist, nothing done to appeal to the visitor. Tourism has its uses, but it can mangle a city, especially a developing city, and flatten it into a permanent shape of service: the city's default becomes a simpering bow, and its people turn the greyest parts of themselves into colourful props. In this sense, Lagos has a certain authenticity because it is indifferent to ingratiating itself; it will treat your love with an embrace, and your hate with a shrug. What you see in Lagos is what Lagos truly is.

And what do you see? A city in a state of shifting impermanence. A place still becoming. In newer Lagos, houses sprout up on land reclaimed from the sea, and in older Lagos, buildings are knocked down so that ambitious new ones might live. A street last seen six months ago is different today, sometimes imperceptibly so – a tiny store has appeared at a corner – and sometimes baldly so, with a structure gone, or shuttered, or expanded. Shops come and go. Today, a boutique's slender mannequin in a tightly pinned dress; tomorrow, a home accessories shop with gilt-edged furniture on display.

Admiralty Road is cluttered, pulsing, optimistic. It is the business heart of Lekki, in the highbrow part of Lagos called The Island. Twenty years ago, Lekki was swampland and today the houses in its estates cost millions of dollars. It was supposed to be mostly residential but now it is undecided, as though partly trying to fend off the relentless encroachment of commerce, and partly revelling in its ever-growing restaurants, nightclubs and shops.

I live in Lekki, but not in its most expensive centre, Phase 1. My house is

CHIMAMANDA NGOZI ADICHIE was born in Nigeria. She is the author of the short story collection *The Thing Around Your Neck* and the novels *Purple Hibiscus, Half of a Yellow Sun*, which was named the 'Winner of Winners' over twenty-five years of the Women's Prize for Fiction, and *Americanah*, winner of the National Book Critics Circle Award. She is the author of three non-fiction books, *Dear Ijeawele, or a Feminist Manifesto in Fifteen Suggestions*, *We Should All Be Feminists*, based on the author's TED Talk of the same name, and, most recently, the autobiographical work *Notes on Grief*. A recipient of numerous awards and honours, including a MacArthur Foundation Fellowship, she divides her time between the United States and Nigeria.

MAGODO

OREGUN   ORISIGUN

Murtala
hammed
rnational
Airport

ORUBA

AGBOYI

GBAGADA

SOMOLU

Third
Mainland
Bridge

Lagos Lagoon

TINUBU

SURULERE

MAKOKO

Admiralty Road

Nigerian
National
Museum

Chevron
Nigeria
Lagos Site

IJORA

Banana Island

Lagos Island

Port of
Lagos

IKOYI

LEKKI
PHASE I

LEKKI
PENINSULA II

Tincan Island

Victoria Island

Lekki
Market

ke Island

Calabash Island

EKO-ATLANTIC

Lekki
Conservation
Centre

Beecroft Point

GULF OF GUINEA

0   1   2 km

NIGERIA

farther away, close to the behemoth that is the oil company Chevron's headquarters. A modest house, by Lekki standards. 'It will be under water in 30 years,' a European acquaintance, a diplomat in Lagos, said sourly when I told him, years ago, that I was building a house there. He hated Lagos, and spoke of Lagosians with the resentment of a person who disliked the popular kids in the playground but still wanted to be their friend. I half-shared his apocalyptic vision; he was speaking to something unheeding in Lagos's development. Something almost reckless.

So forward-looking is Lagos, headlong, rushing, dissatisfied in its own frenzy, that in its haste it might very well sacrifice long-term planning or the possibility of permanence. Or the faith of its citizens. One wonders always: have things been done properly? Eko Atlantic City, the new ultra-expensive slice of land reclaimed from the Atlantic Ocean, has already been mostly sold to developers, and promises Dubai-like infrastructure, but my reaction remains one of scepticism. I cannot stop imagining the ocean one day retaking its own.

My house had required some arcane engineering, sand-filling, levelling, to prevent the possibility of sinking. And during the construction, my relatives stopped by often to check on things. If you're building a house you must be present, otherwise the builders will slap-dash your tiling and roughen your finishing. This is a city in a rush and corners must be cut.

Lagos has an estimated population of 23.5 million – estimated because Nigeria has not had a proper census in decades. Population numbers determine how much resources states receive from the federal government, and census-taking is always contested and politicised. Lagos is

THE MAKOKO SCHOOL

It was May 2016 when the Nigerian architect Kunlé Adeyemi won the Silver Lion at the Venice Architecture Biennale for his design for an innovative floating school in Makoko, one of Lagos's largest slums. Home to more than 100,000 people living in shacks built on stilts over the polluted lagoon, the neighbourhood is nicknamed the 'African Venice'. Just a week after the award, the school collapsed following an unremarkable storm. Makoko is an area not officially recognised by the local administration and therefore at risk of uncontrolled evictions, given the constant need for space and new homes. The school, which was intended as a symbol of redemption for the shanty town, had been inaugurated in 2013. It was a triangular structure made almost entirely of wood, resting on a base of around 250 floating plastic barrels. There were three levels: the first was a meeting place and playground for adults and pupils, with two floors of classrooms above. Adeyemi capitalised on the inspiring nature of the project, presenting it all around the world and earning himself a reputation as a visionary, but rarely did he or the media outlets that gave him publicity touch upon the fact that the school, as well as not being in use, was quite impractical and had clear safety issues. After its collapse Adeyemi downplayed the significance, stating that it was just a prototype to be perfected, a stage in the journey towards what became the Makoko Floating System, which has also been used elsewhere. Meanwhile he continues to celebrate it on his website.

Shoppers and street traders
in Balogun Market, Lagos.

expected to become, in the next ten years, one of the world's mega-cities, a term that conceals in its almost triumphant preface the chaos of overpopulation. Nigeria is Africa's most populous country – one-in-five Africans is Nigerian – and Lagos is Nigeria's commercial centre, its cultural centre, the aspirational axis where dreams will live or die.

And so people come. From other parts of Nigeria, from other West African countries, from other African countries, they come. Skilled workers come from countries as far away as South Africa while less-skilled workers are more likely to come from the countries that share a border with Nigeria. My gate man, Abdul, who has worked with me for six years, is a striking young Muslim man from the

Republic of Niger, Nigeria's northern neighbour. In his small ancestral village, Lagos was seen as the city of shining lights. He longed to leave and find work in Lagos. To live in Lagos and return twice a year with the sparkle of Lagos on his skin. Nigeria is to Africa what the United States is to the Americas: it dominates Africa's cultural imagination in a mix of admiration, resentment, affection and distrust. And the best of Nigeria's contemporary culture – music, film, fashion, literature and art – is tied in some way to Lagos.

If Lagos has a theme it is the hustle – the striving and trying. The working class does the impossible to scrape a living. The middle class has a side hustle. The banker sews clothes. The telecommunications analyst sells nappies. The schoolteacher

'Nigeria is to Africa what the United States is to the Americas: it dominates Africa's cultural imagination in a mix of admiration, resentment, affection and distrust.'

organises private home lessons. Commerce rules. Enterprising people scrawl their advertisements on public walls, in chalk: 'Call for affordable generator.' 'I am buying condemned inverter.' 'Need a washerman?'

Perhaps this is why corporations are not viewed with the knowing suspicion so common in the West. 'Branding' is a word entirely free of irony, and people use it to refer even to themselves. 'I want to become a big brand,' young people brazenly say. Big companies adopt state schools and refurbish them, they organise deworming exercises in poor areas, they award prizes to journalists. Even the too-few green spaces in public areas are branded, a burst of beautiful shrubs and plants defaced with the logo of whatever bank or telecommunications company is paying for its upkeep.

ᴧ

This is a city of blurred boundaries. Religion and commerce are intertwined. Lagos has a Muslim population but, like all of southern Nigeria, it is a predominantly Christian city. Drive past a gleaming modern building and it might be a bank or a church. Huge signboards advertise church programmes with photos of nicely dressed pastors, and on Sundays the city is as close as it can get to being traffic-free, because Lagosians are at rest, back home from morning service. Pentecostal Christianity is fashionable, prayers are held before corporate board meetings, and 'We thank God' is an appropriate response to a compliment,

or even merely to the question, 'How are you?'

This Christianity is selectively conservative, it glances away from government corruption, preaches prosperity, casts ostentatious wealth as a blessing and disapproves of socially progressive norms. Women are to submit to their husbands. Hierarchies matter. God wants you to be rich. But it also unites Lagosians; people who attend the same church become surrogate families, and together they attend large vigil services more exciting than music concerts, where urbane men and glamorous women sing praise-songs deep into the night and in the morning return to their well-paid jobs in the high rises of The Island.

In Lagos, ethnicity both matters and doesn't matter. Lagos is ancestral Yoruba land and Yoruba is spoken widely, but it is also Nigeria's polyglot centre, and the dream-seekers who have come from all parts of the country communicate in Nigeria's official language of English and unofficial lingua franca of Pidgin English.

Some areas are known as ethnic – the Hausa sector where working-class northern Muslims live, the areas with large markets run by people from my own south-eastern Igbo ethnic group – but none of them are affluent. With wealth, overt appeals to ethnicity retreat.

My cousin lives in a lower middle class area, heavily populated by Igbo traders. Once, on my way to visit her, the car stuck in traffic, a hawker pressing his packs of chewing gum against my window. Gabriel

Security officers working for the Lagos Central Business District
pose for the camera in Broad Street, Lagos.

A successful evangelical pastor in Nigeria has to be charismatic, skilled at writing sermons and, above all, good at making converts – in other words, customers prepared to express their faith by paying a tithe of a tenth of their income in the hope of obtaining material goods in exchange. There is no scandal, however: the pastors preach that faith will be rewarded in this way and are also successful examples of this teaching, because the money that ends up in the coffers of their churches enriches the ministers themselves. And when a congregation of 50,000 makes donations, sometimes far beyond what they can afford, as is the case at the Faith Tabernacle in Ota, Lagos, those coffers can become very full indeed. The churches' earnings, which are not subject to tax as they are religious organisations, are used to fund companies that develop the faith around the world. A case in point is the Winners' Chapel. Behind its pastor David Oyedepo, who preaches at the aforementioned Faith Tabernacle, is an international empire that also owns a university in Nigeria, one that is beyond the reach of the majority of his followers because of the prohibitive cost. The minister owns private jets and homes around the world and took it as an insult when his personal fortune was estimated at $150 million: not high enough. But millionaire pastors (and extremely influential ones to boot) are not a rarity in Nigeria. Besides Oyedepo there are figures such as Chris Okotie and Chris Oyakhilome as well as the late T.B. Joshua. Almost all of them own TV networks and publishing houses that spread their teaching.

my driver of ten years said to me, 'Ma, your bag.' A simple reminder. I swiftly moved my handbag from the back seat to the floor, pushed it under my seat.

My cousin was robbed in traffic on her way home from work, a gun to her head, her bag and phone taken, and beside her people kept slow-driving, face-forward. And now she has a fake bag and a fake phone that she leaves on display in her front seat whenever she drives home, because robbers target women driving alone, and if she has nothing to give them they might shoot her.

My brother-in-law was also robbed not far from here. He was in traffic on a bright afternoon, his windows down, and someone shouted from the outside, something about his car, and he looked out of the window and back to the road and in that brief sliver of time a hand slid through the other window and his phone was gone. He told the story, later, with a tinge of admiring defeat. He, a real Lagosian who had lived in Lagos for forty years and knew its wiles and its corners, and yet they had managed to fool him. He had fallen for the seamless ingenuity of Lagos's thieves. To live in Lagos is to live on distrust. You assume you will be cheated, and what matters is that you avert it, that you will not be taken in by it. Lagosians will speak of this with something close to pride, as though their survival is a testament to their fortitude, because Lagos is Lagos. It does not have the tame amiability of Accra. It is not like Nairobi where flowers are sold in traffic.

In other parts of Lagos, especially the

'"Beware of Lagos", I heard often while growing up on the other side of Nigeria. Lagos was said to be a city of shallowness and phony people.'

wealthy areas on The Island, I wouldn't hide my handbag in traffic, because I would assume myself to be safe. Here, security is status. Lagos is a city of estates; groups of houses, each individually walled off, are enclosed in yet another walled fence, with a central gate and a level of security proportional to the residents' privilege. The estates not blessed with wealth lock their gates before midnight, to keep out armed robbers. Nightclub-goers living there know not to return home until 5 a.m. when the gates are opened. Expensive estates have elaborate set-ups at their entrances: you park your car and wait for the security guards to call whomever you're visiting, or you are given a visitor's card as identification, or you are asked to open your boot, or a jaunty guard walks around your car with a mirror lest you have a bomb strapped underneath.

In a city like Mumbai, which is as complicated as Lagos, it is easy to understand why the expensive parts are expensive just by driving through them, but in Lagos one might be confused. Mansions sit Buddha-like behind high gates but the streets still have potholes, and are still half-sunken in puddles during the rainy season and still have the ramshackle kiosk in a corner where drivers buy their lunch. High-end estates still have about them an air of the unfinished. Next to a perfectly landscaped compound with ornate gates might sit an empty lot, astonishingly expensive, and overgrown with weeds and grass.

*

I live in Lekki and dream of Old Ikoyi. British colonial government officers lived in Old Ikoyi starting in the twenties, a time of mild apartheid when Africans could not live there and could not go to the 'white' hospital, and could not apply for high-profile jobs. Today, Old Ikoyi has about it that stubborn, undeniable beauty that is the troubled legacy of injustice. With its leafy grounds, and trees leaning across the streets, it reminds me a little of my childhood in the small university town of Nsukka, an eight-hour drive from Lagos: quiet, restful frangipani trees dotting the compound, purple bougainvillea climbing the walls.

And so I find myself wishing I lived in Old Ikoyi and mourning its slow disappearance. Gracious columned houses are being knocked down for tall apartment buildings and large homes with unintentionally baroque facades. 'Beware of Lagos', I heard often while growing up on the other side of Nigeria. Lagos was said to be a city of shallowness and phony people. There were many shimmering, mythical examples of this, stories repeated in various permutations, with the characters from different ethnic groups, and small details changed: the suave man who drives a Range Rover but is penniless and lives on the couches of friends; the beautiful woman who parades herself as an accomplished business person but is really a con artist. And who would blame them, those self-reinventors so firmly invested in their own burnished surfaces?

Clockwise from top left: People passing through the crowded Computer Village IT-accessories market in Ikeja, Lagos; boys preparing shawarma, a popular street food; a girl navigating her boat along a canal in Ilaje, Lekki, Lagos; street vendors hawking their wares in Idumota, Lagos.

MADE IN NIGERIA

When it comes to fashion, Chimamanda
Ngozi Adichie has clear ideas; for public
appearances she wears only clothes by
Nigerian designers. This is a choice that
helps her to promote a sector enjoying
strong growth in her country, while wearing
creations that put her at her ease because
they are designed in a cultural context
with which she can identify and for people
with dark skin, unlike Western fashions. In
Lagos high fashion is growing along with
the number of new designers who apply
traditional fabrics to the demands of an
ever-wealthier and better-educated middle-
class female clientele that is becoming
ever more emancipated. A case in point is
Amaka Osakwe with her brand Maki Oh,
which designs clothes for the 'middle-class
Nigerian girl going on a booty call', seductive
but also protective, for customers who live in
a profoundly patriarchal society with chaste
attitudes to sex, at least on the surface. And
at the same time the designers' creativity
helps to develop the production capacity
of the artisans who sew the garments, so
the whole fashion system benefits. And yet
Nigerian garment production is at risk: the
middle classes mainly wear apparel made
in China, although the clothes transported
from Guangzhou to Lagos are made
specifically by Nigerians for Nigerians to
conform to a specific look, Versage. These
brightly coloured, ostentatious clothes, which
imitate the classical styling of creations by
the Italian fashion house Versace, taking
nouveau riche tastes to the extreme, are an
example of the syncretism and appropriation
at work in the Lagos melting pot.

Above: A tailor works on a client's
dress at his shop in Obalende.
Opposite: Girls having their
photograph taken in a park on Victoria
Island during the Christmas holidays.

Here, appearance matters. You can talk your way into almost any space in Lagos if you look the part and drive the right car. In many estates, the guards fling open the gates when the latest model of a particular brand of car drives up, the questions they have been trained to ask promptly forgotten. But approach in an old Toyota and they will unleash their petty power.

Snobbery here is unsubtle. Western designer logos are so common among elite Lagosians that style journalists write of Gucci and Chanel as though they were easily affordable by a majority of the people. Still, style is democratic. Young working-class women are the most original: they shop in open markets, a mass of secondhand clothes spread on the ground under umbrellas, and they emerge in the perfect pair of skinny jeans, the right flattering dresses. Young working-class men are not left behind, in their long-sleeved tucked-in shirts, their crisp

traditional matching tunics and trousers. And so Lagos intimidates with its materialism, its insolence, its beautiful people.

A young woman told me that when she was considering entering the Miss Nigeria beauty pageant she decided not to try out in Lagos, even though she lived there. 'Too many fine babes in Lagos,' she said. And so she went to Enugu, her ancestral hometown, where she believed her chances were better.

Young people complain of the dating scene. Nobody is honest, they say. Men and women perform. Everyone is looking for what is shinier and better. 'Why do you choose to live in Lagos, then?' I once asked a young woman. Every time I ask this of a young person dissatisfied with Lagos, they invariably look puzzled to be asked, as though they assumed it to be obvious they would never consider leaving. Everybody complains about Lagos but nobody wants to leave. And why do I live here? Why didn't

I build my house in Enugu, for example, a slow, clean, appealing city in the south-east, close to where I grew up?

It is clichéd to speak of the 'energy' of Lagos, and it can sometimes sound like a defensive retort in the face of the city's many infrastructural challenges. But Lagos does have a quality for which 'energy' is the most honest description. A dynamism. An absence of pallor. You can feel it in the uncomfortable humid air – the talent, the ingenuity, the bursting multi-ness of everything, the self-confidence of a city that knows it matters.

The only real functioning Nigerian port is in Lagos, and business people from all over the country have no choice but to import their goods through there. Nigerian business is headquartered in Lagos; not only the banks and the tele-communications and oil and advertising companies, but also the emerging creative industries. Art galleries have frequent exhibitions of Nigeria's best artists. Fashion Week is here. The concerts are the biggest and noisiest. Nollywood stars might not shoot their films in Lagos – it's too expensive – but they premiere them in Lagos. The production of culture works in service to Lagos's unassailable cool.

There are some things of conventional touristic appeal. The last gasp of Brazilian architecture in the oldest parts of Lagos, houses built by formerly enslaved Africans who, starting in the 1830s, returned from Brazil and settled in Lagos. The Lekki market, where beautiful sculptures and ornaments blend with kitsch, and where the sellers speak that brand of English reserved for foreigners. The National Museum with its carefully tended flowers outside the building and inside an air of exquisite abandon. The Lekki Conservation Centre, a small nature reserve, with bounteous greenery and some small animals. The first time I visited, with a friend, I asked the ticketing person what we might hope to see. 'No lions or elephants,' she said archly. The highlights are the gorgeous birds, and the monkeys, and the sheer surprise of an oasis of nature in the middle of Lagos's bustle. The nearby beaches are dirty and overcrowded but the beaches one reaches by taking a speedboat across the waters are clean, dotted with beach houses and flanked by palms.

The restaurants in Lagos are owned by a Lebanese 'mafia', a friend once told me, only half-joking. Nigeria has a significant Lebanese presence. They very rarely intermarry with Nigerians, and I sense in some Lebanese employers a unique scorn for their Nigerian staff, but their roots in Nigeria are firm. They are Lebanese-Nigerians. And they own many restaurants, and their mark is obvious in the ubiquity of the shawarma. Young people go out for a shawarma. Kids ask for shawarmas as treats.

There are, of course, Nigerian-owned restaurants. The chains with basic, not untasty food, the mid-level restaurants that dispense with frills and serve the jollof rice one might have cooked at home and the high-end restaurants that labour under the weight of their own pretensions. There are quirky shops that cater mostly to a new Lagos tribe, the returnees: young people who have returned from schooling in the US or Europe with new ideas, and might for example suggest that a thing being 'handmade' was remarkable, as though hand-making things was not the Nigerian norm. They represent a new globalised Nigerian, situated in Nigeria, au fait about the world.

*

It is the breathing human architecture of Lagos that thrills me most. For a novelist, no city is better for observing human beings. On Sundays, when the roads are not clogged up, I like to be driven around Lagos, headed nowhere, watching the city.

Past bus stops full of people with earphones stuck in their ears. A roadside market with colourful bras swinging from a balcony, wheelbarrows filled with carrots, a table laid out with wigs. Fat, glorious watermelons piled high. Hawkers selling onions, eggs, bread. In gutters clogged with sludgy, green water and cans and plastic bags, I imagine the possibility of a clean city. Lagos is full of notices. 'This house is not for sale' is the most common, scrawled on walls, a warning to those who might be duped by real estate shysters. Near a mosque, where a fashionable young woman in jeans and a headscarf walks past, is this in green letters: 'Chief Imam of Lagos Says No Parking Here'. From a bridge, I look across at shirtless men fishing on flimsy canoes. The secondhand books spread on low tables have curled covers, copies of *Mastering Mathematics* beside *How to Win Friends and Influence People*.

On these drives, I think of how quickly fights and friendships are formed in Lagos. A yellow *danfo* bus has hit another and both conductors have leapt out for a swift fight. People make friends while queuing – at banks, airports, bus stops – and they unite over obvious jokes and shared complaints.

At night, there are swathes of Lagos that are a gloomy grey from power cuts, lit only by a few generator-borne lights, and there are areas that are bright and glittering. And in both one sees the promise of this city: that you will find your kin, where you fit, that there is a space somewhere in Lagos for you. 🐦

THOSE WHO STAY BEHIND

MAITE VERMEULEN

Translated by Diane Schaap

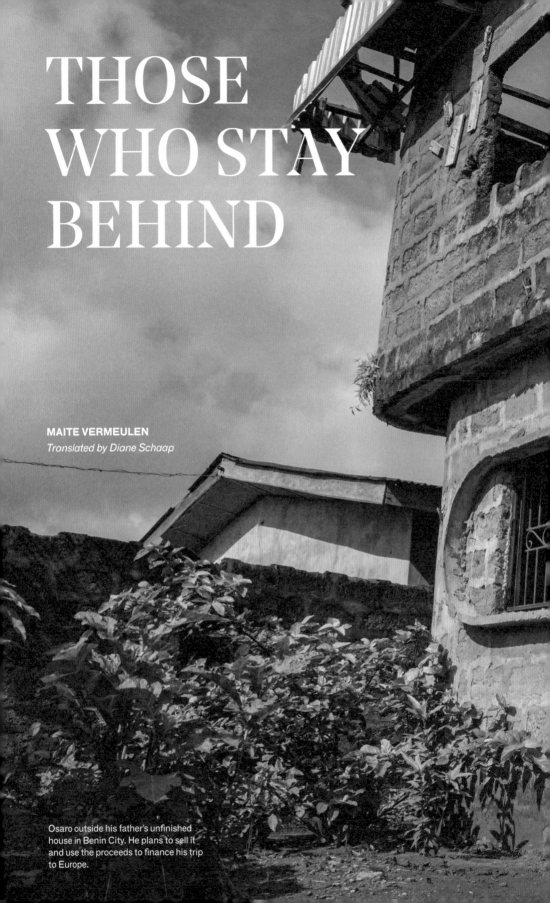

Osaro outside his father's unfinished house in Benin City. He plans to sell it and use the proceeds to finance his trip to Europe.

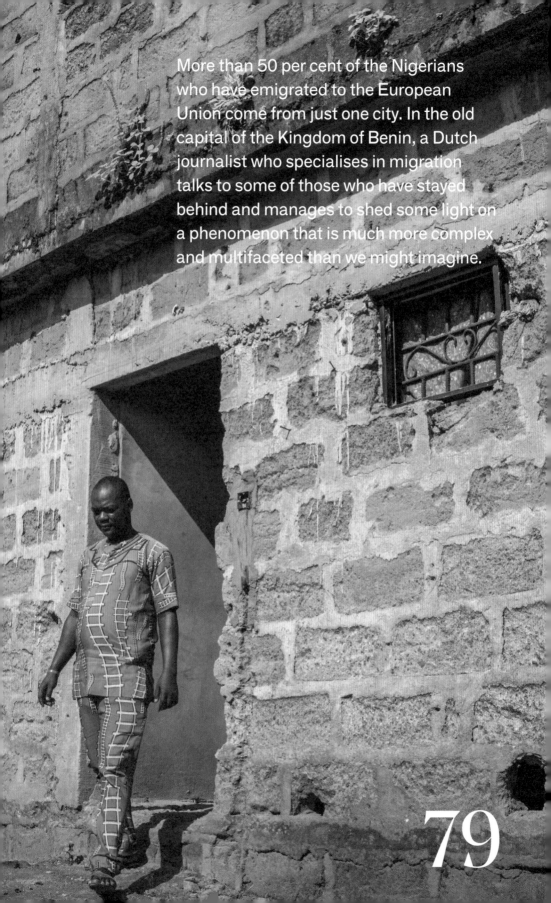

More than 50 per cent of the Nigerians who have emigrated to the European Union come from just one city. In the old capital of the Kingdom of Benin, a Dutch journalist who specialises in migration talks to some of those who have stayed behind and manages to shed some light on a phenomenon that is much more complex and multifaceted than we might imagine.

79

I walk down a muddy road, past wooden stalls full of bananas and smoking barbecues laden with suya, a few high-rise buildings, lots of unpaved roads, a cacophony of car horns, street vendors hawking their wares on every corner. On the surface, there's nothing special about Benin City, Nigeria. But something extraordinary is going on in one of Nigeria's bigger cities. You won't find a single person here without a family member in Europe.

The majority of Nigerian migrants in Europe come from this city of fewer than 1.5 million people. It is as though every Mexican immigrant in the US were from, say, Tijuana. The largest group of African migrants in Europe is comprised of Nigerians – although it would be more accurate to say that Edos or Binis, natives of Benin City, make up the largest group.

I am here to learn about one of the most complicated issues in European politics: migration from Africa to Europe. I want to look at migration from an African perspective – from the perspective of Africans who leave and, more specifically, from the perspective of those who stay behind. I have spent months here, talking to old people, young people, rich people, poor people, people with and without

a job, with and without an education, and – without exception – people whose everyday lives are intimately affected by migration to Europe.

The issue is many times more complex than I could ever have expected. In Benin City nothing is as it seems. It is a place where the categories that we Westerners use to help us understand migration are irrelevant. Trying to understand the issue, it is as though you're turning a prism in your hand, the colour constantly changing as the light hits a new angle.

THE CITY THAT EUROPE BUILT

I walk down the muddy road with Omo, a slender man with bright eyes who grew up here. The house we're headed to can't be missed. It is two storeys, painted a fresh bright green and towers above the low, corrugated roofs of the neighbouring houses. 'Thank U Mummy' is chiselled into a black plaque above the Ionic columns that frame the arched door.

Omo, who works for a local NGO, points to the palatial house. 'Here you see the revolution.'

Europeans would never call the horrific trek through the Sahara and the drifting boats on the Mediterranean Sea a revolution. But here in Benin City it's different.

MAITE VERMEULEN is a Dutch reporter and one of the founding editors of the online magazine *De Correspondent*, reporting on stories from across the globe about development, humanitarian aid, international relations, conflict and migration. She moved to Lagos in 2018, where she lived for two years. She previously studied Conflict, Security and Development at King's College London.

'Enter a church, and you'll hear the priest praying, "Your children shall cross in Jesus' name. They shall cross well, they shall not die."'

Signs of the revolution are everywhere. Omo poetically calls them 'testimonies to travel'. 'Proceeds' is the term that's frequently used. Once someone tells you about the 'proceeds', you notice them everywhere. It's as if someone has handed you 3D glasses at the Imax, and the film has snapped into focus. You see what had been invisible: that petrol station is being built with money from Europe; that red Land Rover was paid for in euros; those new hotels are being erected with European money; the little boutiques with fabulous names – 'Glitz 'n Glam', 'Exclusive Choice Collections', 'G-Armany Fashion' – have been set up thanks to European sponsors.

Omo and I go around a corner. Another gigantic house, this one with shiny grey tiles. Must be family in Europe. Further along, a new roof reflects so much sunlight that it temporarily blinds me. Must be euros.

The small stalls with bottles of liquor also sell cases of wine from Italy. The lingerie on display in large piles was discarded by Europeans. The secondhand electronics being sold at the side of the road were sent from Europe. The red-and-yellow vans used for public transport are called 'Belgian buses', a reminder of their country of origin.

Enter a church, and you'll hear the priest praying, 'Your children shall cross in Jesus' name. They shall cross well, they shall not die.'

'The city that you see,' says Omo, 'has been built by Europe.' Not through development aid or investments but by irregular migration. 'If you conduct a poll on the street here,' predicts Omo, 'eight out of ten families will have children in Europe.' His own uncle, aunt and three cousins have 'crossed'. They are now working in Spain and Austria. His grandmother lives in a big house with shiny new floor tiles, paid for in euros.

Omo and I put his theory to the test. And it's true – it really doesn't matter who we ask. The barman, the barber, the receptionist at the hotel. The priest, the taxi driver, the peanut seller on the street corner. Whether they are fourteen or forty-four, male or female; whether they've attended university or just primary school, whether or not they speak English. Everyone in Benin City has family or friends in Europe. And, given the chance, just about everyone would want to go themselves. '[I would go] right away, even without saying goodbye to my mother,' says Sandra, who volunteers at her church. 'Wouldn't think twice,' says Sunny, who is studying at university. Just last year his cousin drowned in the Mediterranean.

Among European Union (EU) policy-makers and migration experts, alarm bells have been ringing for a while about Benin City. The statistics don't lie. Around 60 per cent of Nigerian asylum seekers who arrive in Europe are from Edo State, the capital of which is Benin City. The overwhelming majority come from the city itself, according to the European Asylum Support Office (EASO). A local NGO staffer calls it a 'massive exodus'.

HOW ONE SINGLE CITY CAME TO RELY SO MUCH ON MIGRATION

How can it be that one single state – in effect, one single city – has come to depend so much on irregular migration to Europe?

To understand the present we have to return to the 1980s. At that time Italian businesses were establishing themselves in Edo State. Some Italian businessmen married women from Benin City, who moved back to Italy with their spouses. They began conducting business, trading in textiles, lace and leather, gold and jewellery. These women were the first to bring other women from their families to Italy – often legally, because Italian agriculture badly needed labourers to pick tomatoes and grapes. But when plunging oil prices brought the Nigerian economy to a virtual standstill at the end of the 1980s, many of these businesswomen went bankrupt. The women working in agriculture also had a rough time: their jobs went to eastern European labourers.

Suddenly, many Edo women in Italy had just one alternative: prostitution. This last resort turned out to be a lucrative one. In a short space of time, the women earned more than ever before. And so they returned to Benin City in the 1990s with plenty of European currency – with more money, in fact, than many people in their city had ever seen. They built 'four-flats', houses made up of four apartments, to earn rental income.

The women were called 'talos', or Italian mammas. Everyone looked up to them. Young women saw them as role models and wanted to go to Europe, too.

Researchers call this 'cumulative causation theory': each successful migrant leads to more people from their community wanting to migrate.

Almost no one in Benin City knew where exactly the money had come from.

'DOLLARS ARE NO TABOO'

The talos began to lend money to girls in their families so that they could also travel to Italy. Not until these women arrived were they told how they would repay the loan. Some accepted, others were forced. All of them earned money.

In the early years the secret of the Italian *mammas* was kept within the family. But more and more women paid off their debts – at that time it took about a year or two – and then decided to go for big money themselves. As so-called 'madames', they began to recruit other women in their home city. Then, slowly, the penny began to drop in Benin City: huge numbers of their women were working in the Italian sex industry.

'Yet no one was really offended by it,' recalls Roland Nwoha. He works for Idia Renaissance, an NGO in Benin City dedicated to helping victims of human trafficking. He grew up in the city and saw women he knew depart for Italy. 'Yes, we knew what they did there, but we didn't condemn it. It helped families out of poverty, so it was accepted. In our four-flat lived a family that was so poor that they were three years behind on rent. The landlord threw them out. Their family of seven had to go live in one room in a slum.' Encouraged by her mother, that family's eldest daughter left for Italy. 'Three years later she had sent so much money home that her parents built a two-flat themselves! I remember how shocked I was at the transformation. Now her mother has even opened a small supermarket.'

Emigrants from Nigeria 2005–20

Thousands   ☐ to the EU   ■ to other countries

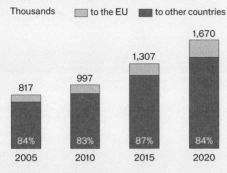

SOURCE: EU ATLAS OF MIGRATION 2021

Remittances by emigrants to sub-Saharan Africa, by country 2021

Because of the pandemic, total remittances to Nigeria plummeted by nearly a third, from $23.8 billion in 2019, dropping from 5.3% to 4% of GDP. Sub-Saharan Africa is the region of the world where commissions for money transfers are highest, equivalent to about 8.5% of the remittances themselves (the UN recommends a maximum of 3%).

Billions of dollars

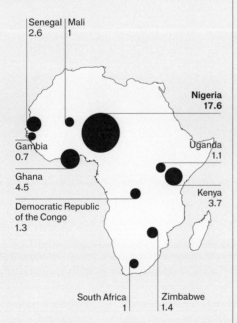

Senegal 2.6 | Mali 1

Nigeria 17.6

Gambia 0.7

Uganda 1.1

Ghana 4.5

Kenya 3.7

Democratic Republic of the Congo 1.3

South Africa 1 | Zimbabwe 1.4

SOURCE: KNOMAD

Asylum seekers in the EU by country of origin, April 2019–March 2020

African countries in bold

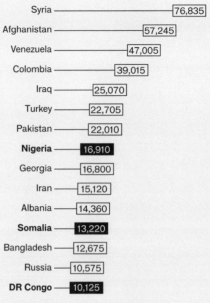

Syria	76,835
Afghanistan	57,245
Venezuela	47,005
Colombia	39,015
Iraq	25,070
Turkey	22,705
Pakistan	22,010
Nigeria	16,910
Georgia	16,800
Iran	15,120
Albania	14,360
Somalia	13,220
Bangladesh	12,675
Russia	10,575
DR Congo	10,125

SOURCE: STATISTA

Oil revenues vs. remittances by emigrants 2014–18

When the price of oil is low, remittances constitute a key source of income for the country.

Billions of dollars

■ Remittances by emigrants
■ Oil revenues

	Remittances	Oil revenues
2014	20.8	42.7
2015	21.2	13.4
2016	19.7	10.4
2017	22	13.4
2018	25.1	18

SOURCE: PWC NIGERIA

Philomona Jombo in front of her house in Benin City.

THE PASSENGER   Maite Vermeulen

'In Benin City, this approach is called the "three Ts": trick, trap, transport.'

'Dollars are no taboo', a Benin City saying goes – another way of saying we couldn't care less where your money comes from. And that remains true today.

There are Western Union and Money-Gram signs all around Benin City, yet much of the money and goods from Europe does not arrive via official channels. On Erie Road is the 'local Western Union', as the people in Benin City call the dilapidated building. The moss-covered block of flats, which also serves as a mosque, has a steep staircase full of rubbish. There is no electricity, so the hallway to the little office is dark. The family that runs this enterprise has 'contacts' all over Europe, where Nigerian migrants can bring money or goods if they pay a commission. With a secret numeric code, their family in Benin City can then receive the money.

A woman in a blue-and-yellow wrapper is sitting against the wall with her head in her hands. Her daughter in Italy hasn't given her a code yet. 'Don't worry, the money will come,' another woman says to comfort her before walking out with two large plastic bags.

TRICK, TRAP, TRANSPORT

The system for getting Edo women into the European sex industry has been fine-tuned over the years. The woman's travel arrangements are made for her, and the costs are paid as an advance. She then has to pay it back with interest. Not until she has paid it back is she free to do what she wants in Europe. The most obvious career choice is often to start recruiting others herself.

In Benin City, this approach is called the 'three Ts': trick, trap, transport. Originally, it went like this:

Trick: tell the woman that she is going to Italy to work in an African supermarket or as a babysitter.

Trap: get the woman to take an oath before a traditional juju priest. For most Edos, this is a life-or-death contract. If a woman runs away or goes to the police after taking such an oath, something terrible will happen to her or her family.

Transport: send the woman off to Europe with a fake visa and plane tickets (which is more expensive, leaving the girl with a bigger debt), or via the Sahara and the Mediterranean. The smuggling networks from Benin City control every step of the journey, from the trucks and rubber boats to the brothels in Italy, Brussels or Copenhagen.

It is often said that the poorest of the poor cannot migrate because migration is so expensive. That is not true in Benin City. All women can migrate *if* they go into debt. 'I see women who can't even write their own name, who have never used a toilet,' says Nwoha. 'They could never get to Europe without help.' And unless they are willing to work as a prostitute. Whereas the Italian *mammas* in the 1990s could keep their profession a secret, now everyone here knows what happens in Italy. Surveys by the University of Benin City Observatory show that almost 100 per cent of respondents know about the work of Nigerian women in Europe.

If everyone knows – and the T for trick is actually redundant – then why do women still go?

For major events, many Nigerians will call on the services of an 'expert', who will use juju to help bring about a desired outcome – for example, during the rainy season, when such practices might be employed to influence rainfall. The belief in supernatural powers and magic (both white and black) is widespread in sub-Saharan Africa, regardless of religious creed, although it often comes down to a person's social class or level of education. The effects of such beliefs, and the contexts in which they are applied, can vary widely, from harmless superstitions you might find anywhere or talismans that protect you against road accidents and other forms of adversity, to rituals that might involve eating a particular animal part, or succumbing to paranoia and stigmatisation. One example of the latter is 'penis theft', or koro syndrome, something that originated in Asia. This affects men who are convinced that their genitals are retracting after having been cursed; cases of lynchings of the presumed sorcerer have been known to occur. Unfortunately it can be one short step from the philosophical position that nothing happens in life by chance to the belief that a malign spirit lies behind every problem. The consequences can be tragic – as when parents, following an illness, a theft or a natural disaster, assume that the cause is that one of their children is possessed and try to drive out the evil or beat a confession out of the child. Wealthier families might employ an exorcist (perhaps from one of the many neo-Pentecostal churches run by self-appointed entrepreneurial gurus who profit from these situations), to deal with this, but poorer families have been known to simply abandon a child.

THE WOMEN ARE PRESSURED INTO PROSTITUTION ... BY THEIR MOTHERS

In a flat on a side street off one of Benin City's busiest thoroughfares, ten women and two babies are sitting around a heavy wooden table. A woman in a garment that most closely resembles a night-dress (shapeless, white, patterned with little ribbons and hearts) is speaking, and the other women uh-huh softly. 'Thomas did not believe that Jesus stood before him until he touched his scars,' says the woman in the nightdress. Her voice is deep. 'Jesus asks us not to doubt. We should believe what is written in the Bible.'

This is the morning prayer at Sister Bibiana Emenaha's women's shelter. Her NGO, Cosudow, offers somewhere for women to stay after returning from European prostitution or, increasingly often, from Libya. The shelter is badly needed. Families will often not take women in because their trip has been a failure. Because they have not earned any money.

The woman in the nightdress asks if anyone would like to share something about the prayer. One of the women – who was in Italy, locked in a room where one man after another had his way with her – sighs, 'People always want to see first before they believe. But we should believe right away.'

Sister Bibiana thinks that is precisely where it often goes wrong. She looks comfortable in her light-blue habit, but her eyes betray her fatigue. 'Ninety-eight per cent of these women know that they will work in Europe as a prostitute. What they do not know is the gravity of what that means. That they will be stripped of every human right, that they will become sex slaves. That their bodies will no longer be their own. They hear the horror stories

'"Ninety-eight per cent of these women know that they will work in Europe as a prostitute. What they do not know is the gravity of what that means. That they will be stripped of every human right, that they will become sex slaves."'

but think, I'll believe it when I see it. That is not my portion.'

Those were the thoughts of 28-year-old Faith – she thought she would work as a babysitter. Instead, she stood at the side of a wooded road near Naples seven days a week for eighteen months. 'I was a slave.'

And then there is the pressure. I speak to Sandra – twenty-nine, petite, an 'I ♥ Human Rights' button pinned to her pink blouse – who is currently looking out for travel opportunities. She says she doesn't want to work in prostitution. 'But I am the eldest of four. My father is deceased, my mother is old. I have to take care of my brothers and sisters. I have to make my mother forget that my father is dead. You can imagine the pressure ...'

Family pressure – often from mothers – is the major reason that women continue to go, according to Sister Bibiana. 'Everyone here is competing to send their child to Europe, to build a house, to buy a car. "Ashawo no dey kill," they say.' Prostitution won't kill you.

In some neighbourhoods there are even clubs for mothers who have daughters in Europe. Not as support groups but as status symbols. Visibly distressed, Sister Bibiana says, 'Mothers here are ruining their own daughters!'

Adesode is one such mother, one who 'encouraged' her daughters to travel. She has ten children, four of whom are abroad. She saves the snapshots they send her in a thick, red photo album. Her favourite is the one of her daughter in a Santa Claus suit. 'Thanks to them, I now have a house with a real fence around it,' she says, pointing to the imposing cast-iron monstrosity.

A few minutes' ride away is the home of Philomona, who has been caring for her grandson in the ten years since her daughter left for Europe. She shows me the extra rooms that have been built with her euros. But when I ask about the work her daughter does, the conversation founders. Philomona begins to stutter, 'She ... she works in a factory ...'

Me: 'What kind of factory?'

'I'm not exactly sure ... A factory in Belgium ...'

AND WHAT ABOUT THE MEN?

For a long time, more women than men migrated from Edo State, but that pattern has changed.

Of those from the state who sought asylum in Europe in 2017, nearly 60 per cent were men. And of those who returned from Libya – those migrants who did not reach Europe – half were men and half were women. For irregular migrants, statistics from the Edo State government even place the ratio of men to women at seventy to thirty.

This is logical: if the smuggling networks are so deeply intertwined with the city, why would men not make use of them? Especially since opportunities for young men in Benin City aren't exactly abundant.

In one of the city's slums, Loveth, a mother of three, runs a small café where a grey parrot speaking Pidgin English entertains customers. Her establishment is mainly a place for unemployed people to hang out. 'Look around,' says Loveth, 'these should be tomorrow's leaders. But where are the jobs?'

The economy of Edo State has tanked in the past decade. Jobs have disappeared left, right and centre. The state bus service went belly up. The state brewery did so poorly that they did not pay any salaries for thirty-six months. Okadas, the motor-cycle taxis, were banned.

Loveth says, 'Here you are seeing grad-uates working as waiters, cement carriers, builders, mechanics. So why would you go to school?'

Edwin (thirty-four) knows that frustra-tion like no other. He has a master's degree in social work but has been doing volun-teer work for years because no one can pay him. To get by, he does the odd building job. He takes me to a gigantic house – surrounded by a wall with watchtowers and a 'God Is Great' plaque – where he laid tiles a few years ago. The house belongs to a friend in Europe. 'That's the funny thing,' Edwin says, his wavering voice betraying the tragicomedy. 'That friend never went to school, and he builds a house. I have my master's, and I lay the tiles. That's the funny thing ...'

Opposite top: Lucky, who works for a paramilitary organisation, in his room in Benin City; he hopes to make enough money to join his father in Europe.
Opposite bottom: Osaro at home in Benin City.

THE BENIN BRONZES

Rather than bronzes these are actually a varied collection of brass plaques, inlaid elephants' tusks, statues and masks; and they do not come from the country known as Benin but rather from the kingdom of the same name that was located in what is now the south of modern Nigeria. The artworks, dispersed among the leading museums of Europe and North America, are currently at the heart of a debate linked to their return; for the people of Benin City, these are not just artefacts to be exhibited but examples of a cultural heritage that is still alive. The objects arrived in Europe with the British soldiers who set out for the Kingdom of Benin on a punitive expedition in 1897, which resulted in a massacre of the population and the looting of the state and its treasures, hastening the kingdom's collapse. A deep wound inflicted on the local culture, as if Europe had been stripped of all its artworks from the Renaissance to modernism, according to the artists of Benin City. And, in fact, the value of these objects to European art is the reason that some collections do not want to give them up; according to some curators the pieces that inspired Picasso and Modigliani should remain where they are now. Fortunately, not everyone is of the same opinion, and some European museums, from Berlin to Ireland, and to a lesser extent also the Met in New York, have begun to return some of the stolen objects to Nigeria. In the meantime, however, fresh controversies have broken out in Nigeria. Two separate museums have been designed to house the objects, one of which is under the control of the royal court of Benin – which still exists – and the other is independent. Both would like to exhibit the entire collection.

Of course, the women are not the only ones who know how to earn money in Europe. The men send money home, too. Frederik has two younger brothers, aged eighteen and twenty-two, who have just crossed to Italy. They haven't been able to find work yet because they are in a detention camp awaiting their asylum procedure, and yet Frederik is already calling their departure an 'enormous relief'. 'They each receive €50 a month from the Italian government. They send that money home. My mother is overjoyed.'

Osamuyi and Osaro are also in Loveth's café. Osamuyi has just returned from Libya, where he stayed for eighteen months in the hopes of crossing to Europe. Twice he got into a boat. Twice he didn't make it. His story terrifies me. In Libya, he was sold as a slave. He watched friends die right in front of his eyes.

His friend Osaro has just sold all his belongings so he can begin the same journey. In his small room just behind Loveth's café, only the mattress remains.

I ask Osaro if he isn't deterred by the stories of slavery and murders.

'No. Whether by land, sea or river, I am leaving this country. There are no opportunities here. I'm fed up.'

I ask if Osamuyi wouldn't advise Osaro to stay here after all of his experiences. 'No, I wouldn't discourage anyone from going. For every five hundred who try, three hundred make it. I had bad luck; maybe he will be lucky.'

BENIN CITY: NIGERIA'S MIGRATION HUB

People here need to get lucky before they even leave Nigeria. Osaro knows that well enough. Among the many smugglers in Benin City, it is pretty difficult to find a reliable 'connection man'. Two years ago his trip failed the day before his departure when his smuggler ran off with his money and that of his seven fellow travellers. Now he has a new connection, via a friend who has already arrived in Germany.

I meet a connection man – or 'boga' – who specialises in filling out visa applications. He actually feels more like a middleman because he doesn't do the falsification of the accompanying documents; he only puts his clients in touch with the 'right people'. He operates from his official business, a hole in the wall where he repairs computers and printers. He is surrounded by dusty devices.

This connection man got his start by helping two family members to get visas for Cyprus and Russia. 'Since then I have not had a moment's rest,' he laughs. 'People from all over Nigeria are beating my door down! This year alone I have already helped fifteen people cross.'

In past decades Benin City has become a migration hub for the whole of Nigeria. Every Nigerian knows that in Benin City

you can find contacts who can help you get to Europe. The entire economy runs on migration, just like in other migration hubs such as Agadez in Niger or Sabha in Libya. Seen through that lens, it is not so strange that Omo calls this migration 'a revolution'. He adds with dramatic flair, '[A revolution] to free us from slavery and the shackles of poverty!'

FIGHTING HUMAN TRAFFICKING
You can imagine that the average family in Benin City is not keen on measures to curb migration.

Around the year 2000, when Roland Nwoha's NGO began a campaign against human trafficking, they became the target of extortion, voodoo assaults and threats. A group of women actually marched, naked, to the king's palace in protest against the NGO. Nwoha says, 'They were furious. They shouted, "Do you want to steal food right out of our mouths?"'

Now, too, there is still plenty of resistance. As the governor of Edo, Godwin Obaseki, says, 'During my election campaign I was told that I was not to talk about human trafficking because it would lose me votes.'

When he was elected at the end of 2016, he did, in fact, start a robust campaign against human trafficking – with the support and encouragement of the EU.

Step one is a brand-new unit: the Anti-Human Trafficking Task Force. The only things in the office are two desks, a refrigerator and some boxes. The walls are still perfectly white with nothing hanging on them. 'There is firm resistance from the communities that now profit from migration,' says Oyemwense Abieyuwa, the secretary of the task force. 'But we must do something. The massive migration is an embarrassment; it makes our state look bad.' The new unit and a new anti-trafficking law now afford the state the opportunity to convict human traffickers, whereas before that was possible only at the national level. The unit is now investigating twenty-eight cases. 'We want to hit them hard,' Abieyuwa says. 'We are showing human traffickers that it's no longer business as usual.'

And that is having an effect. Everyone in Benin City is talking about the fact that many bogas are now in hiding – especially since the king began to get involved in March 2018, putting a curse on human traffickers and forcing traditional priests to revoke the juju oaths of women in Italy.

The question is: who is profiting from this crackdown and the trafficking networks going underground? Experience in other countries, such as Niger, shows that harsh measures do not result in less migration – rather, they lead to higher prices for migrants, greater profits for smugglers, more dangerous routes and

THE OBA OF BENIN

Although Nigeria is a constitutional democracy, the country's hundreds of ethnic groups still hold their traditional tribal leaders in very high esteem. Among the most respected and most influential is the oba, or king, of Benin, a key figure for the Edo people – Edo being the original name for what is now Benin City (and no connection to the modern Republic of Benin). The history of the Kingdom of Benin spans at least a millennium, with its greatest period of expansion between the 15th and 17th centuries, while its slow decline ended with the British occupation in 1897 and the temporary exile of the oba of the day. His descendants still live in the royal palace – which was built between 1255 and 1280 and then rebuilt after 1914 following its destruction at the hands of the British – and

they have not lost their authority, particularly in spiritual matters but in other domains, too. The oba retains a peace-making role in many disputes; although his pronouncements have no legal weight, they can nevertheless be very effective, as in the case of the current oba's edict against juju oaths that bind the victims of human trafficking to their traffickers or to brothel-keepers. Many ceremonies performed by the oba date back over seven hundred years, and on some occasions, such as the annual Igue festival, animal sacrifices are still performed. But Ewuare II, the current incumbent, the fortieth, is certainly no sorcerer. Prior to ascending the throne in 2016 he had served as Nigeria's ambassador to Angola, Sweden and Italy and worked at the United Nations. He has five wives, the youngest of whom has recently given birth to quadruplets. Long live the Kingdom of Benin!

THE PASSENGER   Maite Vermeulen

A billboard on Uselu Road, Benin City, advertising a seminar aimed at people looking to travel abroad.

stronger ties to organised crime. And, potentially, to greater instability.

'The main thing is that we must offer alternatives for earning money,' Abieyuwa says. The governor intends to build factories with international money – for example, for processing cassava and palm oil – to create jobs.

Such long-term development initiatives cannot, however, count on much confidence from the local population. The people of Benin City have seen governors come and go, seeing little change in their daily lives. A local NGO staffer says, 'As long as our system does not work, it does not matter how much development money the EU gives our government. That money does not get to us. But the money of migrants goes directly to those who need it. Migration is the only way to survive here.'

This dilemma is what you see if you keep turning the prism of Benin City. An illegal system that also benefits many. A dehumanising system that is also a lifeline.

YOU CAN'T SIMPLY STOP PEOPLE MIGRATING

In the EU we like to think about migration in terms of neat little boxes. A person is either trafficked or smuggled (and the former has more right to a residence permit). A person is either a victim or a perpetrator (and the latter must be 'broken').

But in Benin City those dividing lines are not firm. They are fluid. It all depends on the angle of the prism. A Nigerian man who hires a smuggler can suddenly become a victim of trafficking in Libya. Women sometimes start out as victims and, once in Europe, become traffickers themselves.

People smuggler, parent, victim of human trafficking – in Benin City one person can fit into all of these boxes at once. And when Europe uses this narrow understanding of migration to inform policy, the industry gets more brutal. In recent years it has become just about impossible for trafficked women to pay off their debts because the costs of their journey are now so high, but, if they recruit five other women, they can reduce their debt by half.

Sister Bibiana sees the effects. During our conversation she keeps fiddling with a Post-it. There is a phone number scrawled on it. All of a sudden, she says, 'I know a girl who has returned from Libya. She has gone mad. She is in a psychiatric hospital. She didn't make it to Italy, but the people who paid for her journey are still demanding that she pay off her debt! I have never heard of that before. How can she possibly pay? Yesterday they beat her up. This is the number of the madame. I have to call her …'

Naturally, taking a tougher line on migration requires more involvement from the authorities, more assistance for victims and that the issue be put higher on the political agenda. But even Nwoha, who fights human trafficking with his NGO, knows that in Benin City every attempt to stop migration amounts to nothing. 'This migration, even though it is human trafficking, lifts so many people out of poverty. You can't simply end it.' 🖎

The Nation Called Ineba

A. Igoni Barrett

From her spartan home in Port Harcourt, the author A. Igoni Barrett's grandmother held together a large family scattered across Nigeria and around the globe without ever making a secret of her desire for at least one of her children or grandchildren to become a doctor, who would 'treat her with dignity and heal her for free' in her old age.

95

There was a time when Ineba, the only grandparent I've ever seen alive, seemed the oldest person I knew. She was always clothed in starched blouses, mothball-scented wrappers and thick-soled slippers, her head-tie knotted like an Easter gift, which she unwrapped indoors to reveal the low-cut hair that marked her out in that era of drippy Jheri curls and bouffant perms. This was in my childhood after my parents' marriage ended, and my younger brother and I were sent off to the home of my mother's mother. Ineba was a widow, a label that evoked storybook crones in our fanciful minds. That was why her voice would switch from warm to frosty at our excited yelps or the thumping of our feet as we frolicked about, and her palm, when it struck your cheek, was as bone-dry as the Cabin biscuits she gave out as treats.

True to her austere nature, Ineba never played 'round and round the garden', the only carer who never stuck their finger up our armpits or blew raspberries into our bellybuttons. She never gave us a birthday gift that wasn't everyday food from her cooking pot; she never marvelled at our pranks or told us a bedtime story.

A. IGONI BARRETT is a Nigerian writer born in Port Harcourt. He made his debut in 2005 with the short-story collection *From Caves of Rotten Teeth*, which includes 'The Phoenix', a BBC World Service short-story award winner. His second collection, *Love Is Power, or Something Like That* (Graywolf Press, 2013) was followed by his first novel, *Blackass*, which was published in the UK in 2015 by Chatto & Windus and Graywolf Press in the USA in 2016.

The photographs of Ineba and A. Igoni Barrett's family are reproduced with the kind permission of the author.

When she felt our absorption in *Danger Mouse* and *SuperTed* – those cartoon series that children across the country hurried back from school to watch on network TV – was destroying our chances of a bright future, she would gripe like *Voltron*'s Haggar all through that day's episode about the importance of being earnest with our homework. I was her first grandchild, and she wanted me to study medicine, to become the first physician in the family, who would treat her with dignity and heal her for free. She drummed this future into my head until I believed it so thoroughly that it took years to throw over the guilt of disappointing her. Over those six years we squatted in her house I came to know her well enough to stop fearing her. Her domestic patterns were the mould in which mine were formed, either directly or through my mother; the way she cooked plantain pottage became my favourite food. I was fifteen and resented adults by the time we returned to our mother, but I always recalled Ineba with fondness whenever her daughter's cooking scented up our new home.

I found out my grandmother's age on her ninety-fourth birthday. She had refused to answer that question for as long as I'd known her, and would say with a stern shrug, 'A lady never tells her age.' For those six years of our parents' absence Ineba had wished my brother and me happy birthday like clockwork (always in the morning after we arose from bed and went over to greet her), and yet we could never return the compliment. Her age and the date of her birthday were a family secret, one left undisturbed out of respect for her feelings. This tradition of silence had been passed down to her daughters – my mother and her three sisters – whose own ages were also a prickly topic. In the family my grandmother created in her image it seemed only sons were celebrated for growing older, while the women, every year, settled deeper into agelessness.

The city in which I was born and where Ineba lived is a gruelling ten-hour journey by road from Lagos, where I've settled for the past fifteen years. I've seen my grandmother too few times in the twenty-five-odd years since I stopped living with her. As is the case with many highly educated Nigerian families, Ineba's children and grandchildren are spread all over Nigeria and around the world for work and school. When these aunties, nephews and cousins caught up with each other on chatting apps, we traded emoji-riddled news about our matriarch's waning health, her cataract blindness and wheelchair-trapped existence, the first signs of memory loss that we suspected to be dementia's onset. She had become a living tale that her descendants told each other to close the distance between them. We'd flown the nest in pursuit of our dreams, but the widow who babysat the chicks, the non-graduate whose adoration of learning had started a degree-seeking tradition in her family, was still living in the same decrepit house in Port Harcourt, on the same street she had moved into forty-some years ago and was now, on her ninety-fourth birthday, finally exposed as its oldest resident.

It started with a phone call from my brother. He had travelled to Port Harcourt for some business, his first trip back there in years. A few days before he set off we had met up in Lagos and agreed that he would visit our grandmother to see if her condition was as we'd heard. The weight of his voice was the confirmation I'd been dreading. 'Big Mama is going,' he said. 'She didn't even recognise me.' He was still on the line when I decided I would fly down. I had put off seeing her for too long. Her self-sufficient spirit and loner's lifestyle, that homebody's habit she had of never visiting for pleasure, only for milestones like weddings, births and deaths, was a pattern now recognisable in my engagement with my maternal family. But that felt a poor excuse for neglecting the grandmother who had only ever asked two favours of me. One was to become a doctor; the other, which she'd phoned me out of the blue nine years ago to speak about (the only time I ever received a call from her), was to use my middle name, Igonibo – it was also my grandfather's, her late husband's name – in full on my book covers. Both wishes had been rebuffed.

But now, on that day in March, hearing my brother speak of her, I was gripped by the premonition that if I postponed my visit beyond that month I would live with the guilt for ever. 'You'll meet me here,' my brother promised after I blurted out my travel plans. And then he ended the call without realising it was my birthday. It was 26 March, the date our grandmother had remembered without fail in those six years we lived with her.

My wife and I arrived in Port Harcourt on the last day of March. It was the second year of the Covid-19 pandemic, and the hassle of air travel was exhausting for us, even on that one-hour flight. But I felt like the clock was winding down, the fire was closing in on that library called Ineba, and so, after a quick stopover at the hotel to drop off our baggage, we pressed on towards the house whose owner was already haunting my thoughts. During that taxi ride I phoned my brother to tell him that I'd landed, only to find out that his work had intervened to undo his promise. He had left Port Harcourt and was unsure if he would return in time for the birthday party. 'Her birthday?' I repeated over the phone in a stunned voice. He knew the date? How long had he known? Who gave up the secret? Surely not her? My questions tumbled out in an effort to make sense of his revelation.

'April second,' my brother said.

My grandmother's birthday is only seven days after mine. In those six years we lived with her she would wish me a happy birthday on every morning of 26 March while showing her gap-toothed smile, and yet she never once let it slip that her own birthday was the following Saturday, or Sunday, or what-ever weekday I happened to be born on that year. Her birthday had shadowed mine throughout my life, a trivial circumstance turned significant by her refusal to acknowledge the connec-tion. It was a clear sign of her fading powers that her secret was being discussed in the open by the entire family. For it turned out, my brother told me, that everyone who could make it down was expected to show up at her house on 2 April for a family reunion at her birthday party. There would be food, drink, a cake with icing and candles and live music from a church trumpeter. There would also be three generations of her bloodline – in person and through video call – gathered together to sing 'Happy Birthday' to her. 'How old is she now?' I asked my brother on that phone call, but the answer would come two days later, after the birthday song had been sung.

*

Ineba's six children had done well in the ways that mattered to her. They each held degrees from respectable universities and had all given her grandchildren, none born out of wedlock. Her eldest daughter, my mother, was remarried to a Briton and lived in London, the same city to which her brother Tony, Ineba's fourth child, had migrated in the early 1990s. He was now a passport-holding citizen of the UK, but his accent hadn't switched its allegiance to Nigeria in his thirty-odd years away. When he visited along with his four children (the two eldest from a white British mother and the others from a sweetheart he'd left behind in Nigeria and then reconnected with after his first marriage ended), the nasal accent of these London-born cousins was always a source of confusion to their grandmother. Yet she still managed to find out, I'm sure of it, which of them wanted to be a doctor when they grew up.

Ineba's second child, who'd earned a degree in law, had only recently retired as a permanent secretary from the Ministry of Justice. In my childhood she was the bonfire of the family gatherings, with her sharp wit, thundering laugh and the ease with which she drew her young nephews into the conversation, never talking down to us. The Law was the only adult who allowed my brother and me to call her by her nickname. But after she married and bore children she turned to religion, a fundamentalist Pentecostalism that transformed her catholic humour into a dogmatic shrillness. In the years after her conversion, every

time I paid her a visit, she was always carping on about the sinfulness of the world, especially as exhibited by her colleagues. She believed no one liked her at her workplace because she was the light and they were steeped in darkness. This explanation was too easy for anyone who had endured her conversation, peppered with Bible quotes and exhortations to turn to Christ. Her second child, who still lived with her in his thirties, had heeded the Word and grown up to become her only begotten convert. But her wild evangelising wasn't as successful with her husband, who'd finally moved out of their home so he could think and drink in peace. Neither had she convinced her daughters. The eldest had left for Canada to attend university and remained there for work, her earnings contributing to the fees of her sister, who had moved to a Caribbean island to study medicine.

Apart from The Law, Ineba had two other children based in Port Harcourt. Both of them, Helen and George, were the mainstays of her comfort in old age. George was her last child and had lived with her since he returned from university some time before my brother and I bade farewell to that childhood home. He had got married in that three-bedroom house, stayed on there with his wife, and his three children had arrived to further cramp the space. He became Ineba's carer as her sight and then her legs began to fail. He took the decisions in her waning years that she'd made for him in his infancy. He handled her money, supervised her feeding, ensured her teeth were brushed and moved her into the smallest bedroom when he needed more room for his expanding family. The few tasks he wouldn't take on included changing her diapers, which was where Helen came in.

Same as her immediate elder sister The Law, Helen was a recent retiree from the civil service. After working for thirty-five years as a secondary-school teacher she was sent home with a modest pension that further restricted her simple lifestyle. Her ex-husband was an oil company exec whose salary had been at least ten times higher than hers. She knew how it felt to live in air-conditioned comfort, but after their separation she'd adjusted to her vehicle-less condition with a contentment only understood by those who have survived an abusive partner. Her serenity bubble-wrapped her against the blows that kept on coming from that abandoned marriage. Their four children had become a vengeful father's only foothold in her life, and for two decades he'd used them like boxing gloves. He flaunted his money at their mother through the gewgaws he bought for them, the game consoles their mother couldn't afford and the high-end smartphones they didn't need, the takeout pizzas and ice-cream jaunts, the obscene sums of pocket money, even through their education, as he insisted on choosing and changing their schools without consulting her. When she complained about their new school's distance from where they lived, he countered by buying a Mercedes-Benz to park over at her house and hired a driver to carry his children – only – wherever they wanted to go. Helen accepted everything she couldn't change and still found a means to raise her two boys and two girls with decency. By the time their father stole them away by enrolling all four in universities outside Nigeria, they were already their mother's creations, forged in the furnace of her unbreakable spirit.

Of all Ineba's daughters, Helen had always lived closest to her mother, even once renting an apartment on the same street corner. She was friends with Ineba's friends before they all died off, and over the years she'd become the repository of her mother's childhood memories and dying wishes. Yet Ineba's favourite child had always seemed to be Kingba, her last daughter. It was she who fulfilled her mother's long-held dream of having a doctor in the family, as she'd married one straight out of university. It was Kingba's romance that revealed a side of Ineba I'd never suspected as a child under her roof.

On that day Kingba had brought over her suitor to meet the family at Ineba's house. The lovers announced their news to happy faces and congratulatory prayers, which filled the house with an

atmosphere that Ineba's growing gang of grandchildren channelled through our uninhibited rowdiness. Later that night, after our playmates and their parents had all departed and we'd been shushed and shooed off to sleep, I awoke to a feeling I couldn't place at first but later realised was the sound of a broken heart. I crept out of bed without disturbing my sleeping brother and cracked open the bedroom door to eavesdrop on the excitement. Mother and daughter were huddled together in the shadows, their voices lowered but distinct. 'You can't marry him,' Ineba was saying as Kingba sobbed. But why not, I must have wondered, before hearing my grandmother proclaim the reason that made no sense to a twelve-year-old.

Ours was a middle-class, educated, city-based and widely travelled Nigerian family. We didn't have ethnic biases so ingrained they smothered love. Or so I thought until I heard my grandmother say that her favourite child couldn't marry her beloved doctor because we were Kalabari and he was Igbo. That was nonsense, of course, because Kingba went on to wed him and bear their three children. There was no hint of scandal about their relationship, no further night-time whispers to disturb my sleep. But my grandmother's words were singed into my memory and had altered my gaze for ever. For it made me question how my brother and I, the offspring of a Jamaican father, fitted into a culture that saw Igbo rather than doctor, ethnicity over education.

Before Kingba's rebellion, all of Ineba's children had married two types, based on place of origin. Kalabari or non-Nigerian. The Law, Helen, Tony in his second marriage and George had all selected partners from their mother and father's minority ethnic group. Love is love, even within that shrinking gene pool called a tribe, one may argue of these recurring happenstances. Then again, coincidences are messages to the blind. Since my grandmother had ripped the veil from my eyes and spilled that inkpot of ethnic colourations into my mind, I had to wonder which of her offspring had been persuaded to shun love in the wider Nigeria.

Two lived abroad, and both had married foreigners, while all six, in their pursuit of university education, had travelled through all the cardinal points of Nigeria and returned unconvinced, except for Kingba.

*

On that last visit to Port Harcourt, my grandmother looked like the oldest person I'd ever met. She was enthroned in a plastic chair when my wife and I slipped into her spartan bedroom. We stooped over her and muttered sweet nothings, our voices struggling to hide our sadness at the price a body pays for its long life. As my brother had reported, her memory was leaking away with each tremulous breath she took. She didn't recognise me or my wife, whose white skin caught her attention for an instant and proved to us that her blindness was not complete. What do you say when all that's left is the drudgery of convalescence? Do not go gentle into that good night, dearest Ineba? I had done my duty and was now ready to leave that house where my childhood memories were losing out to these new impressions. And so I drew closer and inhaled her soap-scented warmth, pressed my lips against the wrinkled, hairless, tender skin of her face and cleared my throat for my farewell spiel. 'Can you hear me, Big Mama? This is Igonibo. I love you, I'm leaving now, but I'll see you again on your birthday.'

My words, for the first time, drew a coherent response from her. She raised her head and stared at me with opaque eyes, her jaw working as she ground her gums. 'Igonibo,' she called out in that same voice that had named me at birth. 'I did something bad to you. I was wrong, I'm sorry. Please forgive me.' And then the undertow of her swirling memories swept her away again, leaving me helpless to interpret the meaning of her plea. *I forgive you, I forgive you, I forgive you*, I chanted on that day as she rocked in her seat to the beat of her ebbing life.

But truly, Ineba, there's nothing to forgive. You were born before Nigeria became a nation, and you raised us, you showed us, you prodded and inspired us, writers and doctors and all those graduates, into living versions of the proud country you wanted. You had your flaws, but, like Nigeria's, they are not insurmountable and can be struck from our constitution so long as we keep the faith and continue to build afresh, one nation bound in freedom. Our founding mother is Ineba, and we are scattered across the world under diverse passports but united by one vision. Treat her with dignity, and heal her for free. 🖋

Postscript: My grandmother Ineba passed away in her sleep on 26 August 2022, about sixteen months after my last visit as described in this essay. Her final gift to her family was to foot the expenses for her funeral through her life savings. That's my Big Mama, fiercely independent to the end.

The Centre for Girls Education, in Zaria, Kaduna State, is one of the few Nigerian NGOs that aim to ensure that girls have access to education, and the centre has safe spaces for girls of all ages. The principal objective is to provide basic literacy and numeracy skills, but adolescent girls are also taught about puberty and the reproductive system.

A Mixed Bag: Being a Woman in Nigeria

Being a woman in Nigeria means being subjected to many kinds of discrimination while simultaneously seeing huge advances in gender politics – but how do these two truths intersect? Writer and lawyer Cheluchi Onyemelukwe interviews women from all over the country in an attempt to understand.

CHELUCHI ONYEMELUKWE

In 2016, upon being asked about potentially damaging statements his wife had made about the administration in an interview, Nigeria's President Buhari notoriously quipped, 'I don't know which party my wife belongs to, but she belongs to my kitchen and my living room and the other room.' Interestingly, Mr Buhari stated this on a visit to Germany while standing next to Chancellor Angela Merkel, the leader of one of the largest economies in the world, who happened to be a woman. This resulted in intense dissections on social and other media, funny and insightful cartoons and distress for many women. For some, it was merely a public spat between a couple in power, the vagaries of politicians, with little significance for the rest of the country. Others saw it as a deserved put-down for a wife who did not understand her place. For many, however, women in particular, it was a reminder that, despite many steps forward, many achievements by women on the national and global stage, gender equality was still a long – some might say very long – way off. It seemed an approach intended to minimise, to gaslight and to diminish all at once. If a president could speak like that about his wife in public, in an international forum, what did it really mean to be woman in Nigeria in the 21st century? Or did it really matter, coming from a former military leader?

The incident reminded me of some of my own experiences of gender-related belittlement. In one instance, it was at a police station. I was visiting my parents in the village with my children in the south-east of Nigeria, as is now our tradition. On the day of my visit the police also came by to drop off a letter of invitation to come in to see them. My father, an economist, a former civil servant and university lecturer, was happy to have his daughter, a lawyer, a university lecturer, around. On the day of the event he took me and another relative to the police station. The divisional police officer would not look at me. I got the impression it was beneath him. He would not direct questions to me, even when my father made it pointedly clear that I was representing him. He looked past me to the other relative and did his best to ignore my increasingly insistent interjections. On account of my father's poor sight, the officer was eventually obliged to let me write down his statement, and

CHELUCHI ONYEMELUKWE is a lawyer, academic and writer. She is the author of *The Son of the House*, winner of the Nigeria Prize for Literature 2021, the SprinNG Women Authors Prize 2020, the Best International Fiction Prize (Sharjah International Book Fair 2019) and finalist for Canada's prestigious Scotiabank Giller Prize 2021. It was named one of the books of the year by Canada's *Globe and Mail*, CBC Books and *Channels Book Club*, Nigeria. She is the founder of the Centre for Health Ethics Law and Development (CHELD), which focuses on gender and gender-based violence in Nigeria and other African countries.

Changing ... politics

NAME: **Ngozi Okonjo-Iweala**

DATE OF BIRTH: **13 June 1954**

PLACE OF BIRTH: **Ogwashi Ukwu, Delta State**

Born into a powerful family near the Niger Delta, after her initial studies in Nigeria she took off for the USA to attend Harvard University, where she graduated *summa cum laude* in economics before gaining her doctorate at MIT in Boston with a thesis on the agricultural development of her home country. Having spent many years working at the World Bank, where she managed an operating portfolio worth $81 billion, she returned to Nigeria in 2003 to serve as finance minister – a pioneering move, as she was the first woman to hold the position. She also became the first woman – and the first African – to lead the World Trade Organization, a position she has occupied since 2021.

it felt as though he had done me a favour – me, a lawyer of over a decade, a senior law lecturer. In another instance, representing a woman who had been abused, I was reminded by a male police officer that a woman needed to respect her husband and that domestic violence was merely a private matter to be settled between a man and his wife or, if he chose, their families. On other occasions, it has simply been a waiter automatically handing the bill to a male colleague or employee after a meal.

A few years after the incident with my father, in 2021, I am sitting in my classmate's office in the centre of Lagos Island. I have come to seek her assistance on a case of violence against women in which my organisation, the Centre for Health Ethics Law and Development (CHELD), is involved. She welcomes us, me and my colleague, and listens to the case as we lay it out. People, women and men, come into the office, present issues and problems, listen carefully to her orders and nod in acquiescence. She is the divisional police officer in charge of the largest and most important police stations in a city of twenty million people.

Are things changing for women in Nigeria? What does it mean to be a woman in Nigeria today? Nigeria's population of around 200 million is almost evenly divided between men and women – 49.3 per cent are female and 50.7 per cent are male – but some might argue that this is the only area of equality between men and women. The World Economic Forum's *Global Gender Gap Report 2021* – which measures several key variables, including poverty, education, health and political participation – ranks Nigeria 139 out of 153 countries on the index, a significant downwards move from 2006 when Nigeria ranked 94 out of 153.

This all sounds academic, so one might wonder what it is really like being a woman in Nigeria.

*

Growing up in a middle-class family in the south-east of Nigeria in the 1980s, there was little to distinguish us at first, boys and girls – we were all children, required to go to school, respect our elders, attend church, wash plates and, when in the village on cold Harmattan mornings, sweep the compounds. We boys and girls built sandcastles together and later went to after-school lessons together. The roles of fathers and mothers were clearly defined: fathers provided; mothers cared and nurtured. There were nuances, however. My friend, whose parents worked in the railway industry, where salaries were often patchy, had to take on other assignments, breed chickens to sell, make clothes on the weekends for clients. There was an unspoken rule about being presentable. And there were more rules about closing your legs and learning to cook. Some rules applied across the board, whether you were poor or rich.

Our parents expected us to do well, and, if I recall correctly, there were just as many girls as boys getting good marks in exams. Later, when I went to university, I do not recall there being any conversations about which courses were best suited to males or females. It was expected that we would do well, come into society and be productive, fending for ourselves and our families. It was not quite so straightforward, of course. There was the question of marriage, which is where the paths often diverged.

In school we were taught about Mungo Park and his so-called discovery of the River Niger, on the banks of which many people had lived long before his arrival. But we also learned about the many men who fought for independence – Nnamdi Azikiwe, Obafemi Awolowo. At home I read books, a wide range of which my father kept on shelves around the house. One day he bought a set of three large hardbacks – these were books on Africans who had shaped their countries and the continent in the 20th century. They had short summaries of men from Chad, Niger, Zimbabwe, Kenya, Zambia, Cameroon and others, who had fought wars for their countries, stood boldly against colonialism and for the independence of their nations, become the first doctors, lawyers and so on. The women across all African countries were only a handful, apparently too few of them had done things impactful enough to merit a space in the ample volumes.

It seemed to my little-child's eyes that, despite no specific dictum in this regard at school and at home, the men did the important things, the things that stood out. All the governors whose names we had to recite were men. All the ministers who served in the cabinet of the head of state were men. It was also borne out by what most of us saw at home, fathers who had high-up jobs and mothers who had jobs, too, but often less exalted ones and seemingly earning less money. Our mothers did the really important things – taking us for tetanus shots when we hurt our feet, as we often did running about, taking us for back-to-school shopping, making sure there were meals for everyone, whether they cooked it themselves or relied on other females to do so. These are generalisations, of course, and there were differences in some families, although not different enough to alter the general picture.

But I also learned about a few outstanding women who had done extraordinary things, fewer than the men, for sure, but still extraordinary. We learned

Changing ... the story

NAME: **Mo Abudu**
DATE OF BIRTH: **11 September 1964**
PLACE OF BIRTH: **London, UK**
NICKNAME: **Africa's Answer to Oprah**

'If you don't take the responsibility to change the narrative, when you leave your storytelling to someone else, then you can't blame them': this was Mo Abudu's takeaway from her interview with Hillary Clinton in 2009 on her talk show *Moments with Mo*, which is distributed all across Africa by her own TV channel, EbonyLife. Today, having built her empire up from nothing, she is one of the world's most influential women in the entertainment sector, and she recently signed a historic agreement with Netflix to produce films and TV series under the US streaming giant's brand but in Nigeria with Nigerian stories, subjects and characters. All this in spite of what she describes as triple discrimination: because she is Black, African and a woman.

Changing ... health

NAME: **Temie Giwa-Tubosun**
DATE OF BIRTH: **4 December 1985**
PLACE OF BIRTH: **Ila Orangun, Osun State**
NICKNAME: **The Blood Lady**

While studying in the USA, she witnessed a woman giving birth during a period back in Nigeria that led to the realisation that there was a need to facilitate blood transfusions to reduce mortality rates for women in childbirth, which were still extremely high in Nigeria. So in 2012 she founded the One Percent Project, an NGO that promoted blood donation. Four years later she realised that making donated blood available to patients dispersed across the vast nation would only be possible with a different business model, one that could cover the distribution costs. To achieve this she founded LifeBank, a company that distributes medical products to Nigerian hospitals, for which she has achieved international recognition and was described by the World Economic Forum on Africa as a positive model for the Fourth Industrial Revolution.

Adaku Okonji (**top**) in her furniture store in Asaba, Delta State, which she has run successfully for ten years (a rare feat in a male-dominated industry); (**below**) a woman shows off her handmade basket at her farm in Gembu, Taraba State.

Adebisi (**top**), assistant director of pharmaceutical services at University College Ibadan, in the university dispensary, and (**below**) the lawyer Altine Sambe outside her home.

about Funmilayo Ransome-Kuti, a politician, the first woman to drive a car in Nigeria, who worked with other politicians such as Azikiwe and Awolowo to throw off the shackles of colonialism and who was the mother of Fela Ransome-Kuti, the legendary Afrobeat musician; she died after being thrown out of a window by Nigerian soldiers. We also learned about Flora Nwapa, Africa's first female novelist; thanks to my father, who started me off, I read almost all her books. It appeared that women came in singles, shining, unique; a few could be extraordinary among several outstanding men. None of this was exceptional, I suppose. Throughout history, and across the world, women have had to play catch-up.

Still, at the high end, women in Nigeria are not doing badly, some might say. My children now in school are learning about extraordinary women who have done outstanding things in Nigeria and on the global stage. Sometimes I worry that some key women are not taught about as often as I would like: Dora Akuniyili, the former medicines chief regulator for the country; Grace Alele-Williams, who became the first female vice-chancellor of a Nigerian university; Nigeria's first female (and so far only) chief justice, Aloma Maryam Mukhtar CJN; or the heroine, Dr Stella Adadevoh, who in 2014 took steps that helped prevent an explosion of Ebola in Nigeria's most populated city and in the process paid with her life. Currently, Nigeria has eight women, the highest number of females ever, leading the top banking institutions in the country. What they all have in common is often being the first women in spaces previously dominated by men. There is still room for 'firsts' for women in Nigeria, including having a leading woman's face on the naira banknotes.

*

Once upon a time, when the Sahara was a wet environment infested with mosquitoes, there was a child with great powers ... and a curse. A genetic mutation gave the child greater immunity to malaria, and in adulthood this mutated gene was passed on to their descendants, who, in turn, went on to multiply. But when two of these descendants met and procreated, they each passed on their own mutation to their child, and the combination produced red blood cells with an unusual 'sickle' shape, which blocked the blood vessels. This is sickle-cell anaemia, a chronic hereditary disease that is very painful and sometimes lethal. The condition is widespread in sub-Saharan Africa, where 80 per cent of the world's cases are found. In Nigeria 2 per cent of children, 150,000 a year, are born with the disease, and half of them die before their fifth birthday. The link between malaria and sickle-cell anaemia has been known since the 1950s, but that it could be traced back to a mutation present in a single individual born 7,300 years ago is a recent discovery, one of the first results of the H3Africa programme, a consortium of around five hundred African scientists with the objective of mapping the African genome. The inclusion of African genomes – the oldest and most diversified in existence – in global DNA databases offers researchers the opportunity to study the genetic causes not just of conditions present in Africa, including sickle-cell anaemia, but all across the world, from Alzheimer's to cancer. Waiting in the wings are the pharmaceutical groups that, with African genome data – in some cases supplied by home-grown biotech start-ups – hope to develop the next generation of gene therapies.

Nigerian women come in all shapes and sizes, in different income brackets, from various religious backgrounds and from diverse ethnic groups. My experiences have shown me that all of these impact the experience of being female in Nigeria.

Income group makes an especial difference, I find. I have a reasonable-looking car, and one can tell that, at least to some degree, I am surviving in Nigeria. So on occasions when the police or a road-safety official stops a car I am in as a passenger, the driver will often say, 'Madam, talk to them. Tell them you are in a hurry.' And I put on my Nigerian madam voice to say hello and ask how they are. And it often works; appearances are everything. 'Madam, anything for us?' they would ask, the smile in their voices already accommodating, helpful and unwilling to make my life difficult.

But it is not so for all women. In the course of living and working in Lagos I come across many women living in poverty. One who worked as a cleaner asked me to intervene in her issues with a husband. He was a driver who beat her for not serving the kind of food he would prefer, for not bringing enough money home, for talking back to him. All she had was already being spent on caring for the children, supplementing what little he gave her. Couldn't she leave, I asked her? She said no, she would not be able to pay her house rent in Lagos by herself. It would be more difficult in her parents' home, and they would not be happy to see her return, little babies in tow, more mouths to feed and the family pride in tatters. Another cleaner overhearing us made sure to let me know afterwards that my solution – to leave the man – was no solution. I sounded, she said, like someone who lived abroad, not in Nigeria. She did not say that it was drenched in privilege and a lack of understanding, but I got the point. Not too long goes by without a humiliating report regarding women, especially women in poverty. Poverty is itself violence – to women and to men – but for women it is often intricately linked in double layers of gender inequality, humiliation, limited choices and a demeaning existence.

Studies note that poverty, while perilous for everyone, is also gendered. Some reports show that women are much more likely to be poor than men. My experiences bear that out. I grew up around men who seemed to have better jobs – as civil servants, business owners. They rented property; some had their own homes. For the most part, many did not have their wives' names on the property, and we knew of women who were thrown out of homes when their husbands died and male relatives took over.

But I also grew up around my mother, who worked and continues to work now as an academic at the age of seventy, always emphasising that work is important and that making something of oneself is essential. I also grew up with my grandmother, who worked on her farm, processed palm nuts for oil, had many goats and chickens and who demonstrated that hard work was not the purview of men alone. She did not own or drive a car, in part because she had no education. In her time, girls in the south-east, but also in other parts of Nigeria, were not sent to school – it was considered too much of a burden for a woman who would be married off to another family.

While some women did really well in farming and other business ventures, limited education and the consequent lack of exposure limited access to income, to other opportunities, to privilege, to respect and to high positions in society. There were exceptional women, of course,

THE PASSENGER   Cheluchi Onyemelukwe

Changing ... style

NAME:
Lisa Folawiyo

DATE OF BIRTH:
5 June 1976

PLACE OF BIRTH:
Lagos

OCCUPATION:
Stylist and entrepreneur

She studied law, but fashion was always her true passion. In 2005 she used her savings to set up the brand Jewel by Lisa, which is now present in Nigeria and New York, selling creations that combine traditional African fabrics with modern designs. She is a central figure in the Lagos scene, where the fashion industry is developing thanks to investments and the establishment of a fashion week. It was a different story in the early days, however; she founded her brand with the intention of going global, but to do so from Nigeria, which lacked infrastructure and a specialised workforce, was a tall order. Today her company and her plans continue to grow, while actresses like the Oscar-winner Lupita Nyong'o wear her clothes on red carpets around the world.

A young woman poses for a portrait at a private resort in Abraka, Delta State.

but in terms of land ownership or socialisation or any number of key issues relevant to wealth generation, this was not a positive thing. We are long past the era when girls did not go to school in some parts of the country simply because they were girls, yet the effects of that time persist today.

If this has changed for many in Nigeria, there are still communities, especially in the north of the country, where girls are married off too early, under the age of eighteen, making Nigeria one of the child-bride capitals of the world and the child-bride capital of Africa. Despite campaigns such as Child Not Bride, the practice persists, engendering a continuing vicious cycle of poverty, a scourge on our collective conscience.

In terms of economic power, females are much more likely to be poor and to bear the brutal brunt of poverty. A recent report prepared by CHELD, covering the intersections of gender with a wide range of issues, found women less empowered on every single economic indicator – education, literacy, financial inclusion.

*

But women who do not live in poverty are not living in paradise either. Gender norms are largely uniform across the country. Across cultures, across religions, men are recognised as superior to women. This understanding is largely undisputed, despite years of work by different development entities and activists. These gender norms remain apparent in leadership structures in communities, in religious organisations and within families. It is accepted by many, even women, that women are/should be subordinate to men – in an interview for this essay, while I was speaking to a woman, a man overhearing me simply said, 'But, madam, a

'One high-powered woman told me how eyes travel down to her fingers, searching for the tell-tale ring to determine just how much respect is due to her.'

man is the head. Even our culture says it. Even if the woman is the breadwinner, she must be under a man.' It was not so much what the man said as the certainty that he was so completely right and the nodding of the head of the woman I was speaking to in acquiescence that made me catch my breath. To both, as to many in this country, it was so self-evident as to be indisputable.

Women are expected to manage domestic responsibilities, take care of children, be submissive in marriage and prioritise their domestic roles over other areas in their lives, including their careers. Men are generally expected to be providers, to take charge of their families as leaders. This requires them to show strength and resilience and suppress their softer emotions. While women are increasingly visible (and successful) in all aspects of life, and men can be generous in 'allowing' women to do these things in a benevolent patriarchal way or progressive in believing that women should be in charge of their destinies, the roles are to a high degree sacrosanct. Even when a man fails in his duties as a provider, as happens, women are often expected to take on these roles circumspectly while maintaining their own duties.

When I speak to women and girls, and they ask how I am able to take on the different roles that I do, I often emphasise the need for a supportive partner who will be blind to the typical nuances of a woman's expected responsibilities. I was lucky to have good role models in my parents, and I was even luckier to find a man who wants me to succeed on

many levels. But this is not as commonplace yet as it should be. Nor does it necessarily obviate the traditional responsibilities that a woman has to take on, even for myself. For some of us in the middle and upper classes, we are able to employ paid help. But the cognitive labour of managing things, often unrecognised and certainly unrewarded, is overlooked. Nor does it completely diminish the derogation in which singleness is held, that marriage for women is not only desirable but essential. One high-powered woman I spoke to as I wrote this essay told me how eyes travel past her face down to her fingers, searching for the tell-tale ring on the correct finger to determine just how much respect is due to her.

Not that long ago there was a hullabaloo about a primary-school text on social and civic studies that taught children that fathers went to work while women stayed home. It was interesting to me, in part because even culturally, at least in Igboland where I come from, this was and remains largely untrue; yes, mothers care for the home, but they often do that while selling their wares – tomatoes, peppers, onions – in front of their homes or while farming their gardens. As the years have gone past, it has appeared to me that to some degree and in some ways we have become more conservative about the roles of women. We can speculate as to the reasons why, but it may take more room than I have here to dig into it fruitfully. Even more so, it simply shows how these norms filter into everything – political leadership, law, employment,

Irate Fawole, director of the nursery school at the Centre for Girls Education in Zaria, Kaduna State (**top**); (**below**) a girl giggles in an out-of-school safe space in the community of Marwa, Zaria.

board diversity and inclusion, reproductive health – limiting women's abilities to work outside the home or earn as much money as men and forcing them to spend significant amounts of time in caregiving and unpaid work. When members of the National Assembly refused to pass the Gender Equality and Opportunities Bill, which aimed to promote the equality of women and men and non-discriminatory practices, these same norms were at play. And when the president speaks about his wife belonging to certain rooms in 'his house', he is speaking a language that is not unrecognised, if not wholly acceptable, to Nigerians.

Our constitution, enacted in 1999, while outlawing discrimination, itself contains certain discriminatory provisions, including that a man can confer citizenship on his foreign-born wife but a woman cannot do the same for a foreign-born husband. And another deems any woman who is married to be of full age for the purposes of renunciation of citizenship regardless of their actual age, which may be below eighteen, effectively infantilising women and giving some legitimacy, however faint, to child marriage. A heated discussion about this provision a few years ago exposed the divisions between the largely Christian south and the mostly Muslim north. The Penal Code Act, which applies in the north of Nigeria where Islam is the predominant religion, provides that a married man cannot be held liable for inflicting injury on his wife where the act is done for the purpose of chastising the wife in accordance with his personal law.

Nigeria has limited numbers of women in elected positions – only nine women in the Senate and thirteen out of 360 in the House of Representatives and just one female governor of a state, and she took over from a deposed male predecessor.

THE INVISIBLE MINORITY

For members of the LGBTQ+ community, it is not easy to live in a country like Nigeria, split between Christianity and Islam, with twelve states governed by sharia law, under which sexual acts between men can punished by stoning. Not only is discrimination not prohibited, the government is openly hostile to the community. Under federal law you can be sentenced to imprisonment for homosexual acts (fourteen years) or even for supporting LGBTQ+ organisations directly or indirectly (ten years). And then there is the 2013 law stipulating fourteen years' imprisonment for those who marry someone of the same sex. These draconian laws are accepted by most of a population that rarely comes into contact with a member of the community – 60 per cent say that they would not accept a homosexual relative. Conversion therapies are still practised, and, although the situation is improving, openly expressing your sexual or gender identity can be dangerous. As with so many things, what makes the difference is representation, the fact of occupying a space, but, as the activist Bisi Alimi points out, it is much easier to be queer when fame protects you: ordinary people are at daily risk of being assaulted. Alimi himself left Nigeria after years of alienation and violence that followed his coming out on live television. Trans people, meanwhile, are practically non-existent, except in the sense of transvestism, which in the north is punishable by a year's imprisonment and a fine.

In fact, the United Nations' Women in Politics report ranks Nigeria 184 out of 188 with respect to women's representation in parliament, one of the lowest in the world, lower than most other African countries, including DR Congo, Liberia and the Gambia. With Nigerian women being very visible on the world stage, successful in many ventures at home, these are head-scratching numbers. Of course, there are certain identifiable reasons behind women's poor political participation – from financial constraints to poor media coverage – but all have some link to gender norms.

These norms show up in other areas, too: single women being denied the opportunity to rent apartments, single mothers being derided and even other areas that one might think of as positive. For example, some businesses prefer female accountants, especially married female accountants – and should this prove puzzling, it is because such women are less likely to make off with money, and, were they to do so, their husbands can be held responsible.

Norms are deeply entrenched, their roots so deep, that even women who seek gender equality and changes in the status quo sometimes believe that such changes should apply to politics and educational opportunities but not to marital or intimate relationships: women retain their cooking roles, while men retain their provision roles. The result is that domestic matters remain firmly female matters, while men have little reprieve from traditional masculine roles. And life in Nigeria does not make it easy to do otherwise. One of the people I interviewed noted that, 'It is too hard to ask women to take on paying bills. Even if you do, you can't force him to cook. Even your family will say you are wrong. So then, you are taking on additional burdens, and for what?' Another told me, 'I don't like the way it is done abroad. I like the way we [women] are taken care of here.' The ways in which both women and men are socialised is often damaging to the concept of gender equality and women's perception of themselves.

On a different note, these norms also seep into how we use our knees in Nigeria. So when the first female chairman of one of Nigeria's largest banks says, 'I kneel before my husband, despite all my achievements,' many nod their heads in approval and ask what those who raise eyebrows at this have achieved. When a popular actor states that it is not acceptable for men to kneel to propose and that it is against culture, we make some noise about it on social media. It does not appear to be that much different right across Africa, if gender analyses by country are any indication, although there are little nuances here and there and some may be somewhat but not wholly different. At least we can draw comparisons with the president of Tanzania's much-talked about statement in 2021, noting that she still kneels before her husband.

*

Violence, I think, deserves a whole section to itself because it tears at the very fabric of being human, dehumanising with no relief especially when there is support, however covert, however insidious, from society. It destroys the spirit as it batters the body. The norms discussed above often show up in violence against women and girls. As a woman who suffered child sexual abuse and later rape in my university days, I am intimately aware of how degrading and diminishing violence against women and girls is.

I often think the statistics do not quite

Countries that treat their women the worst also tend to be the most unstable. Researchers Valerie Hudson, Donna Lee Bowen and Perpetua Lynne Nielsen have developed an index of what they term the 'patrilineal/fraternal syndrome', assessing 176 countries on a scale of 0 to 16 (based on factors such as inequality in law, prevalence of early marriage for girls, polygamy, dowries, violence against women and social attitudes) and have shown that the score obtained is a more accurate predicator of a nation's instability than its income, its degree of urbanisation or the World Bank's Worldwide Governance Indicators.

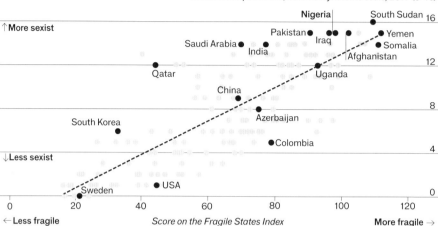

Score on the patrilineal/fraternal syndrome scale, 2017 (0–16)

SOURCE: THE ECONOMIST

capture the horrific impacts, but they are worth stating. According to the Nigeria Demographic Health Survey (NDHS), one in three women in Nigeria has suffered physical violence. In Lagos, for instance, out of 1,329 cases of violence reported in July 2021, 94 per cent were female victims. The NDHS notes that 20 per cent of all women aged fifteen to forty-nine in Nigeria have undergone female genital mutilation (FGM). With the number of girls in the north being married off under the age of eighteen – and with ongoing security issues and conflict in the region exacerbating the situation – young girls risk rape and child marriage. The Chibok girls, who were kidnapped from their school and eventually forcibly married to Boko Haram terrorists, is only the most notorious example of many. Women and girls also constitute the largest number of victims of domestic and cross-border trafficking, with young women from certain parts of southern Nigeria trafficked to Europe for sexual exploitation (see 'Those Who Stay Behind' on page 79).

As in many countries around the world, violence against women and girls, while discriminatory, often does not discriminate: rich, poor and middle-class women and girls all suffer violence. Although on the decline, FGM persists in some communities, in an attempt to protect the chastity of girls and to deny them sexual pleasure. In many homes, emotional and financial violence reign and do not get as much attention as physical violence, and sometimes this is enabled by religious organisations. Women are beaten for burning food, for not taking proper care of the home, for not being sufficiently respectful or for no reason at all. In my organisation, where we mainly support victims of domestic violence, we see how damaging a wide range of violence can be and how limited the resources are for supporting survivors. There are too few shelters, few funding avenues to support women who have been kept out of work and seek to leave situations of violence, among other gaps in the system.

Recent years have seen an increase in those seeking accountability, with many women's groups rising up to challenge the status quo. Several sexual assault referral centres have been established across the country to support victims of sexual assault. Laws have been enacted, principal among them the 2015 Violence Against Persons (Prohibition) Act, which prohibits a much wider array of offences than the Criminal Code. There are many policies – including the one I helped draft, the National Policy on the Elimination of Female Genital Mutilation in Nigeria – but there is still a long way to go.

*

It is not all doom and gloom, however. Nigerian women are shining lights in and outside the country. On the global stage, there is Ngozi Okonjo-Iweala – former managing director at the World Bank, Nigeria's first female finance minister and the world's first female director general of the World Trade Organization – and Chimamanda Adichie, the award-winning writer, being perhaps the most prominent (see 'Still Becoming' on page 63). And there are many others in academe, literature, film, technology, medicine, business and development. Every so often we celebrate a Nigerian woman's success in and

Changing … sexuality

NAME: **Iheoma Obibi**
DATE OF BIRTH: **7 August 1965**
PLACE OF BIRTH: **London, UK**
NICKNAME: **Madam Butterfly**

While taking a course in communications policy studies in London, she asked herself what systemic and educational factors were needed for a woman to occupy a high-profile position. She tried to find an answer by founding Women in Governance (WIG) in Nigeria, an organisation that organised public-speaking classes and looked for female talent in local communities. Today she continues to pursue her activism while also focusing on her company, Intimate Pleasures, which, as the country's first online sex-toy retailer, is at the heart of a revolution in Nigeria. Obibi is also studying to be a sex therapist to bring ever greater knowledge to the afternoon education and discussion sessions for women that she runs in Abuja. Nicknamed Madam Butterfly, when she was asked if she had encountered any obstacles in her career, she replied laconically that she did not think there was enough space to list them all.

especially outside Nigeria, at Harvard, at NASA, at the British monarch's award of MBEs, in Canada, somewhere around the globe.

When I won Africa's – and one of the world's – richest book awards, the Nigeria Prize for Literature, in 2021, one of my uncles told me that, 'There must be something special about being a Nigerian woman.' There is recognition, then, that women have the capacity to lead, to be outstanding, in different areas and ventures. There is a sense that being a woman in Nigeria includes the ability to do extraordinary things and that the platform for such extraordinariness comes directly from Nigeria, from its air, its loudness, its earth, its *swag* and audacity. Sometimes these make men scratch their heads and ask: what more do women want? This, in itself, is worth an analysis: why are Nigerian women doing so well? And then: why is this not more widespread?

The women who are doing well on the global and national stages are most often very well educated. Many have gone to the best schools in Nigeria and elsewhere – the Ivy League in the USA, the top universities across the world. They have won scholarships or they have simply come from well-to-do backgrounds, where their families could afford to send them to the best schools. Living in the diaspora is a plus but not a must. They often have good networks consisting of women and men who have power, and not only political power. Many had and continue to have encouragement from their families. Like me, they were told they could do anything, reach any heights. Like me, many did not know ceilings existed until they went out into the world. With the internet, it is becoming easier to become a phenomenon even if one lives in Nigeria. Many of these women have had to work harder than most men to

Changing ... tyres

NAME: **Sandra Aguebor-Ekperuoh**
DATE OF BIRTH: **1970s**
PLACE OF BIRTH: **Benin City, Edo State**
NICKNAME: **The Lady Mechanic**

Fascinated by cars and engines since she was a child, she managed to overcome her family's resistance to alternate school studies with a mechanic's apprenticeship before graduating in mechanical engineering and earning her licence to repair cars, the first woman in Nigeria to do so. She then founded the Lady Mechanic Initiative, a programme designed to break down stereotypes and help struggling women by encouraging (and teaching) them to work in traditionally male sectors. Aguebor offers tutoring, a small salary, accommodation if necessary and a company placement at the end of the course to deprived women who have often been working since childhood or who have been sexually exploited. The initiative has been hugely successful, and the women mechanics are much appreciated for their professionalism and are finally being taken seriously in a world that was traditionally a male preserve.

A young girl walking through the waterfront community of Marine Base in Port Harcourt, Rivers State.

Saving ... the world

NAME: **Ameyo Stella Adadevoh**

DATE OF BIRTH AND DEATH: **27 October 1956–19 August 2014**

PLACE OF BIRTH: **Lagos**

OCCUPATION: **Endocrinologist**

In the summer of 2014 Dr Adadevoh, last in a line of scientists in her family, having graduated from the University of Lagos and specialising in endocrinology in London, was heading the medical team at a Lagos hospital when she recognised the symptoms of Ebola in a high-profile patient, a wealthy Liberian lawyer. Resisting pressure from his country, she refused to exempt him from quarantine, which she managed to implement in spite of a lack of equipment and personnel – with the case coinciding with a Nigerian doctors' strike – by erecting wooden barricades. The result was that the Ebola epidemic ended swiftly in Nigeria, but not before infecting Dr Adadevoh herself. She died in quarantine in August 2014 and received numerous posthumous distinctions: Abuja named a street after her and Nollywood made a film about her life.

prove themselves. Each breakthrough is celebrated intensely not only by women but by men, too – we are ambitious people, and it is a reminder of what we can achieve and who we can be.

*

Have these successes changed Nigeria, Nigerian thinking on gender norms, subordinate roles for women? The short answer is, not entirely. There is no doubt that it is encouraging, that many young women see in these women what they can achieve, how they can shatter glass ceilings. But, while the successes are brilliant and beautiful at the top, there are still obstacles on the ground, still many barriers to gender equality.

Even for top professionals, sometimes working in male-dominated fields, it is not easy to raise lone voices, in testosterone-charged rooms where there is sometimes a determination to ignore one. One of my interviewees, a high-powered career woman, lamented being described as 'strong' and 'brave'. It is not easy to be hard all the time, a top female professional told me. Sometimes you want to relax and be yourself, but this is rarely possible.

One might argue that my experience with the police officers may be a question of time changing things. There may be some truth to that. But those who know the country well know that we have had women in senior positions in the police and other law-enforcement agencies for many years – but they continue to be significantly fewer in number than men. One might also argue that in a country where there are divergences of religion and culture from one state to the next, and even from one community to another, that these might have an impact on what it means to be a woman in Nigeria. Police officers in Lagos, for instance, are much

> 'One high-powered career woman lamented being described as "strong" and "brave". It is not easy to be hard all the time, a top female professional told me.'

more respectful of issues of domestic violence, but one in three women still faces physical violence, and the laws are still not wholly protective of them; women in political power are still few, and marriages are still not always arrangements of support or partnership. There is progress, but it is incremental and slow.

Social media has been a forum for celebrating these women but also a location for gender-equality conversations and a platform for women (and men) to dissect what it means to be a woman in Nigeria. Men sometimes say that Nigerian women are doing well, at least almost as well, if not quite as well, as the men. Others have argued that women should be prepared to share bills and not simply rely on men, husbands, boyfriends, etc. to 'provide'. The 'gender wars' as some have called them carry a number of hashtags, #wifenotcook #husbandnotATM or the more recent #alphamale. The conversations often emphasise enduring social norms that restrict women to playing a subordinate role and suggest that women still have a long way to go to stand shoulder to shoulder with men in an evolving, challenging society. They can also lack nuance and empathy. But these conversations also show women living boldly, highlighting a different way of being in the world. It would be interesting to see what kinds of changes will occur in another decade. The conversations are sometimes enlightening, other times disheartening, often insightful.

It's all muddy and interesting and frustrating being a woman in Nigeria. In some ways Nigeria is emblematic of the world: the humanity of women continues to be debated in different ways and to different degrees. Sometimes I forget, as I move about doing my work. I see women thriving and finding themselves in the best-of lists of everything. Other times I am reminded that, regardless of how high one climbs in Nigeria, one is hardly ever wholly free of reminders that being a woman is not necessarily equal to being accorded the rights and privileges that are due our male counterparts.

Women in Nigeria are by no means homogenous. Our experiences clearly vary across education, religion and income groups. Many women, like myself, excelling at what we do, would prefer not to be seen as 'victims' and less and less as 'firsts'. But many others struggle with other inequalities that make the challenges of womanhood in Nigeria an extra burden.

In the end, being a woman in Nigeria is a mixed bag, and, in the face of this, most women, as the character Nwabulu notes in my novel *The Son of the House*, are often to be found 'doing their best in their world'.

And that sometimes means trying to change it. ✒

Seeing
Is Believing

KÉCHI NNE NOMU

On the set of *Beautiful Scars* in Asaba, Delta State, in January 2022.

The Nigerian film industry is second only to Bollywood in terms of annual production figures, but its origins and characteristics are very different from those of its international cousins.
In a country with few cinemas, the films – which embrace kitsch, ignore conventions and aim solely to entertain – were distributed initially on videocassettes, something that turned out to be a crucial factor in the industry's development.

133

A Bedford lorry drives through the main streets of a Nigerian town. The vehicle bears on its odd-shaped visor the word 'Ogunde' in bold green letters that are, despite the grain and glitch of the rare documentary film available on YouTube, easy to read. The name belongs to the first known Nigerian-run theatre company, which would, in a few short years, turn to filmmaking. Word on the street is a new show is coming to town. An announcement blares out, as the truck makes its way through an open-air market and past residential houses with street doors, repeating, 'Come to Hotel Frontier. Seeing is believing.' The announcer is seated in clear view, with a microphone, varying the phrasing on the fly as he goes. It's all rather festive.

The scene described above is 1950s Nigeria, likely, and Ogunde's men are scouring the streets for an audience: women, children and men seeking a good time. Later, this jumble of people, mixed in with area boys and onlookers attracted to the scene, possibly bored by other available leisure activities, will idle their time away at the Royal Cinema, Glover Hall, the Road House Cinema or one of the many others spread across the country's commercial centres. It is hard to say what types of films fascinated Nigerians at the time, but among the Hollywood films already beginning to dominate global cinemas and the slim pickings of local films by the Nigerian Film Unit, it is likely that some may have opted to see *Fincho* (1957), the first Nigerian film shot in colour. It is possible that it caused a stir. The film was made by the Latvian-Jewish director Sam Zebba and starred actors considered at the time non-professional by international standards. The film's dialogue, dubbed by Nigerian students at the University of California, Los Angeles, blends Yoruba, Pidgin, British English and Igbo in a multilingual style that must have been unheard of then.

While *Fincho* made its first run in cinemas, Hubert Ogunde, his publicity truck and his troupe made their way through the towns and villages renegade style. On occasion they would do a show in one of the big-city cinemas. The way that it is told by people who remember, the reception given to tepid films such as *Fincho* paled in comparison to the headiness of Ogunde's theatre shows. Around this time, in the late 1940s, the Nigerian Film Unit had been set up to give the colony some control over film production. This unit had the task of creating audience-specific programming to inform the colonial subjects without necessarily giving them access to ideas that could radicalise them. When their cinema vans toured villages, towns and cities they showed mostly documentaries of anthropological activity. Hubert Ogunde and his actors, in contrast, were an insurgency. In small-town hotels and high-end cinemas like Glover Hall, they showed realistic folk operas that wove narratives around the triumphs of daily life, depicting scenes of resistance to colonial rule, the increasing influence of the unions. The operas profiled the rise to prominence of

KÉCHI NNE NOMU is a Warri-born Nigerian author. Her writing has appeared or is forthcoming in *Narrative Magazine*, *Poetry Northwest*, *Boston Review*, *Electric Literature* and *The Sun* magazine. She is a 2022 Narrative Poetry Contest finalist. She holds an MFA in poetry from New York University, where she received support as a Stein-Brodey Fellow, and teaches at the University of Virginia.

revolutionary political figures. And people came to see them in great numbers, filling the halls where they set up shop.

One can attempt to trace a line from Ogunde to the emergent strains of Nollywood in the late 1980s and early 1990s, but the integrity of this claim would be contestable. The protégé–master traditions that defined early Japanese filmmaking, where cinematic cultures like the *shoshimin-eiga* were created and preserved, evident in the style of the Shochiku film studio and the relationship between its founding director Yasujiro Shimazu and assistant/student Yasujiro Ozu, are not immediately apparent in Nigeria's early cinema. What survives of the Ogunde years are a list of his operas domiciled in an online repository and a documentary film published on the YouTube page of the filmmaker Tunde Kelani, a pre-Nollywood old-timer.

*

In the 1970s, during a brief oil boom, cinemas flourished in Nigeria. A small group of filmmakers were having a good run, and Hubert Ogunde began to make feature-length films shot on celluloid. The movies this class of filmmakers made were well received and relatively high grossing, but the boom was short lived against the backdrop of coups and dictatorships, and it was television that really held sway over Nigerians.

People waited for their TVs to come alive in the late afternoon. In any home where there was a television set, there was a rehearsed sequence: dials tuned, antennas set against static to show a glitchy screen and then long minutes waiting for the announcer to come on and read the programme for the day.

The true stars of the 1970s and 1980s were television anchors and local soap opera or sitcom actors in shows that aired some time between the news at seven, the news at nine and the end of the day's transmission. In star power they competed with the enigmatic dictators who could interrupt regular programming on a whim to announce a coup and give the details of a new regime. Only the flamboyant first ladies of the dictators and the occasional political dissident could match them. And they – dictator, first lady and dissident – were often a package deal. On Saturday nights a foreign movie would be shown. On Sundays films that fell under the catch-all term 'matinee' slowed the afternoon if there was no power cut, but the matinees did not hold viewers quite as spellbound as the TV shows and news anchors.

Around this time, too, just as fast as they had spread, the cinemas began to die out. Many of the older, pre-oil-boom establishments – run in their glory days by Lebanese, Syrians, Indians and a couple

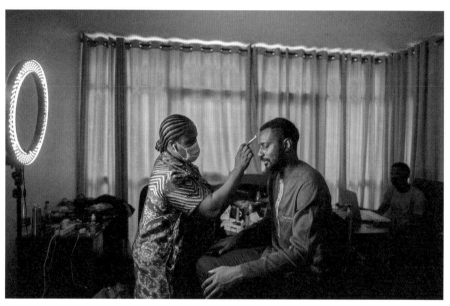

This is the climate in which the film-makers who would create the definitive template for Nollywood began to dream up the home-video form, eclipsing the very niche industry of formalists who, sporadically, continued to make films on celluloid that had to be screened on film projectors.

The enduring image of the Nollywood movie-maker is now one of the bullshit peddler making fast deals with businessmen in the backroom offices of their 'and sons' companies. The product: cheap, ill-conceived films shot on very lean budgets at record speed. But early practitioners of the form were romantics. They shot on shoestring budgets and made their films straight to video, but their idealistic portraits of Nigerian life sought to capture a nation in stages of decline. What they made was half art, yes, but art all the same.

Of the films made by this school, *Rattlesnake* (1995), Amaka Igwe's debut, is now considered a noir classic. It told the coming-of-age story of Ahanna, a sheltered teenage boy from a working-class family whose descent into crime confirms the extent of societal decay around him. He loses his father while his uncle canoodles with his mother and lays claim to his father's small estate. Forced to provide sustenance for his siblings and protect their innocence, he turns to the streets and embraces its vices.

of Nigerian businessmen – had for years been going out of business. Local newspapers would report the rise to infamy of a new robbery gang, and, without fuss or fanfare, the last standing cinema hall in some town would shut down and be sold off. In some cases, the buyer was an ambitious, freshly minted evangelical pastor looking for a large enough auditorium to contain a teeming mass of new religious converts.

With the brief years of economic boom over, and with the cost of living going through the roof, thieving gangs began to pull off legend-making heists and break-ins in the safest of neighbourhoods. Nightlife became too precarious. But people who could afford to orchestrate their own entertainment, and did not want the risk, got VCR players, stayed at home and embraced the escapism of the Hollywood blockbuster. The people who could not afford Hollywood on demand watched Nigerian television serials such as *Basi and Company* or *Checkmate* and Mexican telenovelas such as *The Rich Also Cry*.

Using this same social-realism template with minor tweaks, often voodoo laced, the Ejiro brothers, Chico and Zeb, presented portraits, in early films such as *Silent Night* (1996) and *Domitilla* (1996), of a society waging futile wars against the degradations that had become a part of life during the dictatorship years. But the brothers, more than Igwe, were fascinated by the workings of Nigeria's underbelly and the interiority of its many archetypes.

Silent Night specifically created the mother mould of the Nollywood supervillain in the character Black Arrow.

*

But, at some point, Nollywood turned to schmaltz. The wholehearted embrace of sensationalism and kitsch reached its peak in the first decade of the new millennium. Production companies mushroomed. The films they made were hard to track, many of them defined by their maximalism and/or taste for really bad CGI. The filmmaker became a hack whose through line was more is more.

Every available square inch of wall space advertised Nollywood, with film posters plastered collage style. Posters with images of kohl-wearing women stacked with beads overlaid posters with lurid ritual scenes, which overlaid posters for films about campus girls defending their sugar-daddy-funded lifestyles in big cities and run-down Nigerian universities. We became overexposed to every available variant of the historical saga, whether we asked for it or not. This was the best of times. It was also the last pre-social-media decade, a time when people did not have to overthink absurdity or fear getting memeified.

In films with easily interchangeable plotlines, held together by an associative logic that did not commit to clear narrative arcs or even reality, filmmakers went to absurd lengths to keep Nigerians entertained. The films they made were moral with a side of fairy tale and voodoo. When the films attempted to reconstruct history, research and accuracy were damned. The margin of error was wide and liberties were taken. There was no pretence of originality.

In one film, a man goes blind while taking a bath, and we are made aware that this was the doing of his conniving wife, keen to see that he and his wealth remain under her control. In another – with a different actor, or maybe the same one, and a similar script – the man's 'spirit' would be exorcised, miniaturised and confined in a bottle. This done by a scorned ex or wife to keep him from self-actualisation. For most of the film's duration, in dramatic irony, he would be made oblivious and trusting until a charismatic preacher shows up to reveal the mysteries behind his lost job, house foreclosure, forced evictions, possible body-maiming road accident. All of his miseries traceable to bad juju. Juju and God functioned interchangeably as *deus ex machina*-type devices.

An ode to the industry's dynamism, multiple tropes thrived in the film fauna of the early 2000s right up to the end of the decade. But none of them is as remarkable now as the broad comedies featuring clown-like characters. Many of these took the form of buddy films, the genius of which lay in the fact that most of what happened on screen appeared to be entirely plot free and actor generated with minimal direction. Any actor who could pull off this type of free-form improvisation, rich with banter and one-liners that Nigerians would quickly adopt in their day-to-day conversations, was put in front of the camera. The actors who played these characters were, naturally, typecast to death. Comedic archetypes had, of course, existed in Nigerian cinema and television before this time, but with the invention of the farce, comic Nollywood and its masterminds hit pay dirt.

In *Ukwa* (2001), the first film in this mould, the buddy-film trope had not yet taken shape. The titular character is brought to life by the veteran actor Nkem Owoh. He plays an underachieving man

'In films with easily interchangeable plotlines, held together by an associative logic that did not commit to clear narrative arcs or even reality, filmmakers went to absurd lengths to keep Nigerians entertained.'

The teenage cast of the play *Ogunda Meji* ('The Rejected Stone') at the Seaside Cottage Theater in Bariga, Lagos. The theatre company is a community-based project of the Footprints of David Art Foundation.

steeped too deep in the routines of his life as a village slob with lofty dreams. He is coerced to move to a big city to live with his 'big man' brother. In the city he begins, through myriad schemes, to assert himself, because he is convinced and increasingly bothered by the fact that his place in the world is contested. His ill-conceived actions cause him to be ridiculed, but none of these humiliating circumstances brings him any closer to self-awareness or his version of fulfilment.

Ukwa was so well received that it spawned franchises. Production companies often made versions of this character with spin-offs. The most enduring of the farce comics in the years following were Aki and Pawpaw, the character names of the star actors in the film *Aki na Ukwa* (2002) played by Chinedu Ikedieze and Osita Iheme, a pair of actors recognisable for being little people of something over one metre twenty in height. In the films they starred in together, they were routinely typecast as brothers, friends and each other's arch-enemy. Or they were paired with other village jesters. They riffed off one another on screen and found themselves in fantastical situations, each more impractical than the one before.

Nollywood's rise to global prominence is synonymous with the emergence of a consumer with a distinct taste for these types of mongrel films. The kind of viewer that the romantics made movies for had undergone many waves of metamorphosis by the time the disaster artists and the farce comedies arrived on the scene. Nigeria had become a democracy. The class divides between the haves and the have-nots had now become less defined. Everyone had VCR, CD and DVD players. Cable television would arrive a few short years later, with dedicated channels showing Nollywood melodramas, voodoo

films, blood-money epics, telenovela-style love stories and sagas. Preferably all in one film. The people who made up this broad church of consumers often had all the necessary devices to entertain themselves and mobile phones on the go with bootlegged versions of any film they wanted to see.

*

In 2012 the *New Yorker* writer Emily Witt spent some time in Nigeria shadowing directors and showrunners and attending movie premieres. This was a period when movie-going in Nigeria was making a comeback, and a few cinemas had opened their doors for business, screening a mix of Nollywood and Hollywood films. On a press tour to promote the book detailing her experiences, *Nollywood: The Making of a Film Empire* (Columbia Global Reports, 2017), she told the PBS journalist Elizabeth Flock that the apparent low production quality – or, as she puts it in the book, Nollywood's 'falling short of conventions' – did not appear to deter its most ardent consumers. The films, to use Soviet cinema legend Sergei Eisenstein's words, amounted to 'unmotivated camera work', but most Nigerians did not seem to mind.

To the uninitiated, Nollywood can overwork the senses. It is not for everyone. Its tastemakers, the greater majority of Nigerians who determine what becomes a hit movie, seem to have elected to be entertained by melodrama without undue preoccupation with film conventions. There are Nigerians who long for a future Nollywood where joy, consternation, grief or pain are conveyed with more subtlety on screen, but they appear to be a minority. The average Nigerian cinemagoer will, given the choice, hedge their bets on this Nollywood misadventure

On the edge of Osogbo, a city of around 200,000 people in the south-west, you can visit perhaps the last remaining example of a sacred grove linked to the Ifá religion, practised predominantly by the Yoruba. This spiritual system is based on threefold devotion: to Olodumare (the supreme creator), to the Orisha spirits and to the ancestors. Yoruba settlements in the past would all have had a similar grove for ritual purposes, and Osogbo's natural sanctuary is more than four hundred years old. Legend has it that one of the first settlers in the area heard a voice from the river telling him to leave: this was Osun, the deity that inhabited it. The goddess's wishes were respected, and the town was built away from the grove. Today this pact between the river goddess – the bringer of fertility – and the population is celebrated every August at the Osun Festival. Most of these Yoruba places of worship have been lost through urbanisation and hostility from the Islamic and Christian communities, and as a result the Osun-Osogbo Sacred Grove was declared a UNESCO World Heritage Site. It was saved thanks, above all, to the efforts of an Austrian artist, Susanne Wenger, who fell in love with Yoruba culture, eventually becoming an *olorisha*, an Orisha priestess. From the 1960s onwards she worked to restore the sanctuary, establishing the New Sacred Art group of artists, which created numerous sculptures devoted to anthropomorphic deities. Obsessed with the decline of traditional Yoruba culture and practices, Wenger denied her own children a modern Western education, believing that a more time-honoured path would be better for their spiritual wellbeing.

over a halfway decent film if the latter is too self-conscious as a piece of art or threatens to be a slow burn.

In the much-loved films of the 1990s, conventional filmmaking techniques that are expected or taken for granted globally as standard practices are largely absent. The camerawork is rarely subtle in the way it relays information. The sightlines are wonky. The cinematographer is often simply an eye taking in space and activity, assuming no visual supremacy over the viewer. The filmmaker is only enacting the power of a storyteller to catch and hold our attention on the strength of a story.

By contrast, most of the films by the old-timer Tunde Kelani, considered masterful by many Nigerians, would be placed in the category of 'the slow burn' and mostly overlooked. A student of the London Film School, Kelani likely watched the folk operas of Hubert Ogunde as a boy growing up in the 1950s and 1960s. In the early 1990s, as a new wave of independent filmmakers looking to reinvent the form turned towards festivals such as Sundance to showcase their genre-defying art, Kelani set up his own production company in Nigeria and began to make films that paid attention to composition, syntax, style, historical preservation and storytelling. He had worked as assistant director on the 1990 Hollywood adaptation of Joyce Cary's novel *Mister Johnson*, starring Hubert Ogunde and Pierce Brosnan. He cut his teeth on gigs with Reuters and Nigerian television. The films he has made are quite unlike the usual Nollywood fiction. The relationship between cause and effect is not overplayed, the romance in them does not offer the audience an escape from their realities and they climax at the wrong moments without pomp and flair. They are too proper and bore many Nigerians for precisely these reasons. In

THE FIRST BLOCKBUSTER

Legend has it that in 1992 Kenneth Nnebue, an electronics trader, found himself with a stock of blank VHS videocassettes that he had no idea how to sell. Then he hit upon the idea of using them to record a film. Shot in two weeks, *Living in Bondage* is regarded as the film that changed the face of Nollywood. Co-scripted by Nnebue and the actor Okechukwu Ogunjiofor, it is the Faustian tale of a man who sacrifices his wife in a satanic ritual to obtain power and wealth, but, persecuted by her ghost, he is driven insane and loses everything. The use of the supernatural, the big-city setting and the themes of greed and marital fidelity are features that have subsequently been replicated ad infinitum, but, more than anything, it was the business model – the tiny budget (*c.* $10–15,000), videocassette distribution (which was already the favoured distribution method for pirated foreign films), even the cover design (the actors superimposed on a background using Photoshop) – that was imitated. In a country with relatively few cinemas and extremely low purchasing power, selling VHS tapes (and later DVDs) for two dollars was the only way to reach the public. There are no reliable sales figures in Nollywood, partly because widespread piracy skews the calculations, but there is talk of hundreds of thousands of copies. A film's success is measured by the time it spends on display on the stalls at the Alaba electronics market in Ojo, Lagos State. Thirty years on from its release, *Living in Bondage* (which was followed up with a relatively big-budget sequel in 2019, available on Netflix) is still on prominent display.

DVDs of Nollywood films on sale
in Onitsha, Anambra State.

the 1995 political drama *Koseegbe* there are
scenes where the actors speak in the way
that Nigerians are wont to speak at parties,
the gestures are sufficiently effusive, the
slyness of group gossip comes across,
the fashion is appropriately flamboyant,
but likeness is not what is at stake in the
film. Urgency is. It is a fine enough film,
but it is exactly the kind of film that will
not capture the Nigerian imagination on
the scale that the most underperforming
Nollywood brand of fiction achieves with
ease in the same time period, selling up to
fifty thousand copies in official distribution and bootleg copies.

The majority of Nigerians want their
stories hot-hot. For Nigerians in the
minority who notice and cannot overlook
the holes in the plots, strange cinematography choices, laughable soundtracks,
unrealistic characterisations and obvious
continuity failings, the choice is often to
look away or to concern-troll Nollywood
and its supporters. For people caught in
between, they take the apparent failings
of Nollywood on the chin lightly and make
inside jokes about it.

*

The allegiance runs deep for people
who grew up watching Nollywood films.
They remain attached to the tested-and-
trusted template even now. When many
of the films from what is now considered

the golden era were made, their afterlives
were not imagined. Nobody was thinking
about preserving them. But it is precisely
because of this that old Nollywood from
the 1990s and 2000s now lends itself
to nostalgia and to the art forms of the
internet. The kitschiest of the films have
found new lives in meme factories online.
Frame by frame, the old straight-to-home-
video movies are being mined by people
looking to harvest stills, vaporwave clips
and glitch art. Nigerians who have access
to archives of these films create YouTube
channels for them, and people eagerly
await the uploading of a classic. A vibrant
ecosystem is thriving online in which
young Nigerians cosplay hybrid characters
from that era on Instagram and Twitter.
A comedic actor of buddy-comedy fame
recently began to mint memes of himself
from the old films as non-fungible tokens.

In 2002, when Norimitsu Onishi,
a Japanese-Canadian, christened the
Nigerian film industry 'Nollywood' in a
New York Times article, it was meant to be
cheeky. This was months after the release
of *Ukwa*. On the ground, the industry
was chaotic and still fissuring. It made
no pretence to be held together by structure. The naming was simply an attempt
to induct Nollywood as a cultural soft
power. The industry saw in this an opportunity to play up the loosely structured
production companies, distribution outfits
and the guild of actors that made up the
largely unregulated industry as a mono-
lithic powerhouse capable of churning
revenue, open to foreign partnerships and
investments.

The times were changing fast. Many
of the industry's biggest players still
in their prime feared that they had
peaked. Bored with doing business the
old way, Nollywood had also begun to
lose its appeal for its highest-grossing

stars. In interviews they have granted to the national dailies they gave vague projections of wanting to break into the Hollywood market. The ones who could migrated to North American cities to get as close as they could to Hollywood, where many of them fell off the wagon. Some of those who stayed at home were eager to get their acts together and seek out corporate investment from multinationals. They tried their hand at running talent shows and acting academies. They got the government to sign a history-making deal to fund the industry. They formed film partnerships with production companies from neighbouring countries. They realised the huge potential that films made about the Nigerian diaspora held for expanding the market. They also began to envision shooting for the big screen on 16-millimetre and 35-millimetre film cameras.

In 2011 a government initiative to revamp the industry, called Project Act Nollywood, began to give filmmakers, distributors and talent investors access to grants in billions of naira. In 2013 a film adaptation of Chimamanda Ngozi Adichie's Nigerian Civil War novel *Half of a Yellow Sun*, directed by Nigerian playwright and filmmaker Biyi Bandele, was released, having been made using money raised almost entirely by local investors. It had in its starring roles a mix of actors from Nollywood and Hollywood. It was supported both by Nigerian and British production companies.

These days the industry is ripe for the picking. A steady supply of Nigerian films is churned out every year by a new school of filmmakers. Some of them make their way to film festivals and succeed on the merits of their artistry, as was the case with *The Lost Okoroshi* (2019), directed by Abba Makama. The film is a surface-level questioning of the nature and limits of the Nigerian relationship with spirituality, and it is important for how it plays against decades of Nollywood's fascination with enchantment and the supernatural.

Among the new, however, it is Mildred Okwo and the Esiri brothers (Arie and Ochuko) that hold the most promise.

In one of Okwo's most notable works, *The Meeting* (2012), she attempts to bring to life the inner workings of a Nigerian government office presided over by a bureaucracy-loving civil servant, Clara Ikemba, exercising with relish her power to pick and choose who gets to see her boss. The story falters in places, but the characters are mostly well drawn, funny and true to life.

Unlike Okwo, the Esiri brothers are outside of Nollywood in style and the structures on which they rely, as their debut feature-length film *Eyimofe* (aka *This Is My Desire*, 2020) makes its way in the world. Their film, reliant on the narrative and visual styles of the Hong Kong filmmaker Wong Kar-wai, has been shown on the usual festival circuits and in New York's independent film theatre Film Forum. The film has not been made available in Nigerian cinemas or streaming platforms accessible to the Nigerians who turn films into box-office gold, but it is, notwithstanding, distinctly Nigerian in the story it tells of two city dwellers, Mofe and Rosa, whose lives orbit each other, brushing tangentially but never quite intersecting. One character parts with a significant portion of his savings to get a fake passport to escape Nigeria for a promised life abroad. Another agrees to hand over a child as soon as it is born in exchange for passports to Italy. We buy into their desperate, optimistic pursuits even as we know that their dreams will ultimately be thwarted by forces beyond their control.

5

Nollywood
favourites chosen by
Kéchi Nne Nomu

Tunde Kelani
Thunderbolt: Magun — 2001
A young wife learns that she has only days to live after a mysterious virus is found incubating in her body. But there is a caveat: this virus is not biological; it is a spirit virus. Unsuspecting women become infected by it as a punishment for promiscuity. The film blurs the line between myth and fact, is infused with some feminist dialogue and makes gestures towards campy Nollywood, but, remarkably, it proposes new frameworks to allow mythology and Western science to exist side by side.

Izu Ojukwu
'76 — 2016
A fictional rendering of a pivotal moment in Nigeria's post-civil-war history: the assassination in 1976 of military dictator Murtala Muhammed. The film gives context to the events leading up to the attempted coup and the days following the assassination by telling a modest tale about love, friendship and betrayal. It follows the life of a young and dutiful officer who has to make difficult choices.

Ema Edosio
Kasala! — 2018
Kasala! is a picaresque boy-romp movie by one of Nollywood's most promising new female directors, capturing a day in the life of a group of slum-dwelling friends. All are on an individual quest to reinvent themselves, but, in the meantime, they must find innovative ways to live for another day. We watch them rework their personas and learn survival tricks as they go.

Genevieve Nnaji
Lionheart — 2018
A daughter struggles to step into her father's shoes as head of the family's transport business. The film brings together an ensemble cast of beloved old actors and newbies and does a decent job of updating the Nollywood family-drama genre. It is remarkable for being star actress Genevieve Nnaji's directorial debut and the first Nollywood film to be acquired by Netflix.

Chuko Esiri and Arie Esiri
Eyimofe (aka This Is My Desire) — 2020
Two city dwellers, who live in parallel universes but in the same neighbourhood, are both desperate to escape their lives in Lagos. This beautifully shot film weaves very loose narrative strands between these two characters so that their lives intersect tangentially but never quite meet – and that they never meet and never escape the city is what makes the film great. It should be said, though, that the Esiri brothers are independent filmmakers. Although their material is Nigerian, they might not claim the Nollywood label.

A billboard in Lagos advertising a Nigerian film.

A film such as *Eyimofe*, a slow burn by Nigerian standards, would likely do relatively well on a streaming platform accessible in Nigeria. Nigerians, including the ones committed to old-style Nollywood, love to seek out films by Nigerians on streaming platforms and make them trend. Global giants such as Netflix and Amazon Prime understand this and vie for numbers with local streamers and the multiplexes that show low-to-high-grossing Nollywood films made by a spectrum of filmmakers mostly from the new school who have varying levels of expertise.

Many of the films that land in cinemas and on streaming platforms end up performing well. This does not mean they meet the predetermined filmmaking

To use the term Nollywood as a catch-all for filmmaking in Nigeria doesn't tell the whole story. Although some would have it encompass the full range and variety of Nigerian cinema, more frequently it refers just to the boom that began with the home-video productions of the 1990s, dominated by movies in Yoruba and with a geographical base in Lagos and the south-west. Up in the north, in the city of Kano in the federation's most populous state, there is a parallel Hausa film industry with the nickname Kannywood, coined in 1999, that precedes the term Nollywood by three years and in which the first blockbuster, Ibrahim Mandawari's *Turmin Danya*, dates from 1990. In Kano the influence of India's Bollywood is much stronger than in Lagos: music plays a central role, the settings are more rural and the models of behaviour more traditionalist – although never sufficiently! Kano is one of the twelve states of Nigeria in which sharia is in force, and a scandal that blew up over a sex tape in 2007 led to a tightening of censorship, with the Kano State Film and Censorship Board – led by a prominent member of the Izala Society, an influential radical Salafi movement – going after actors, producers and directors, many of whom ended up in prison. Another victim of the moral fury was the surprisingly buoyant market for romantic novels in Hausa, but, the whole of Hausa culture felt the effects, and many consider such censorship as precisely the reason that Kannywood is seen as a subset of Nollywood rather than the other way around.

standards, even if they are significantly better made. However, it means that the conversation about the value of these films is controlled by Nigerians for the most part. For Nigerians who have grown up watching Nollywood, it is a matter of national pride to see Nollywood accepted globally. This does not stop them from subjecting new-era Nollywood films and filmmakers to scathing criticism if they do not deliver on metrics, which include great cinematography and realistic plots, yes, but also the train-wreck quality of 2000s Nollywood films and the story-telling style of the 1990s.

What appears to be outside the control of Nigerians and a source of increasing concern is a new reliance on reality TV stars to drum up excitement and bring in the numbers. These days investors are more inclined to make budgets available that accommodate high-end equipment and slightly longer shoots, but they want eyes on their products. Producers have found a way to commodify Nigeria's new obsession with its reality stars – a brand of fame monster with dreams of grand, unspecified careers and the inexhaust-ible reserves of passion required to sell just about any product to the millions of adoring fans that make up the mini-empires run from their social media accounts. The superfans of Nigerian reality TV stars in this new matrix are the powerbrokers. They will stop at nothing to sustain the reign of a chosen star, including flocking in huge numbers to bump up box-office figures. Within this new order, movie producers recog-nise where power lies and routinely cast the most visible of reality stars in their projects. This is the new Nollywood experiment. It may seem unusual or skewed to the outsider, but it appears to be working. 🐦

Abduction Nation

For years now, northern Nigeria has been held hostage by the scourge of banditry – but who will pay the ransom?

ABDULKAREEM BABA AMINU

Rahila Godwin sits for a portrait in Barnawa, Kaduna State. She lost her arm in 2019 during an attack on her community in Kajuru local government area, south-east of the city of Kaduna, by suspected Fulani herdsmen. Her children were not spared: her son was beheaded, while her daughter was injured with a machete.

On 13 November 2017 I lost two important markers of my life. The first was the very literal death of my father from a sudden cardiac issue that showed up quite out of the blue. It happened during the earliest hours of the very day I was to begin my annual leave, so I drove to Kaduna at first light. I had been a fairly regular visitor to the city of my birth and where I grew up in a childhood populated by some of the most diverse families I've ever imagined to even exist, then or even now. It also helped that it was only a two-hour drive from Abuja, the capital city, which I had made my home for close on two decades now.

The second important marker I lost is Kaduna itself. The city's 'death', although figurative, is remarkably impactful on me and, indeed, on Nigeria as a whole. It has been one of the most important cities in the country for as long as I can remember, historically the political capital of the old Northern Region. Located in the north-west, on the Kaduna River, it was and it remains a major trading centre and a crucial transport hub. It has been called the 'gateway to northern Nigeria' with zero exaggeration, probably due to its rail and road network. An estimated 8.9 million people – myself included – call Kaduna State home. Founded by the British colonial administration in 1900, the city remains influential as home to the headquarters of various political, military and cultural organisations.

Today the city of Kaduna – the whole of Kaduna State, really – has become unrecognisable. Not aesthetically, mind you, as the current governor, Nasiru El-Rufai, is well into his infrastructural renaissance of sorts. The reason is a palpable fear, in rural areas as well as along the highways leading to and from the city, of a most disturbing group of violent criminals called simply 'bandits'. I am adding quotation marks because of my strong belief that these individuals aren't some Robin Hood-type band of merry criminals who steal from the rich and give to the poor. No, these are bloodthirsty murderous thieves, rapists and killers who have paralysed much of the north-west of the country. You know, terrorists.

The way they operate is quite simple, and basically the same wherever they strike. They set up snap roadblocks constructed of rocks, tree stumps or old tyres on their preferred stretch of highway and attack the first few unfortunate vehicles to happen upon them. They open fire on the cars or buses, killing a good number of people and swooping in to scoop up the rest. It is done so randomly that some attacks would see the criminals

ABDULKAREEM BABA AMINU is a Nigerian writer, editor and illustrator. He pens a popular weekly column for the Nigerian newspaper *Daily Trust* as well as a long-running series of editorial cartoons called 'Back-Hand'. Some of his recent writing and illustration work has been published in the graphic-novel anthology *The Most Important Comic Book on Earth* (DK, 2021).

The road that leads to the village of Kwaja in Adamawa State near the border with Cameroon; the population of 25,000 consists mostly of poor farmers, but bandits active in the area kidnap people for ransom.

kidnapping victims as diverse as artisans, farmers and politicians. It is clear that it is fate that chooses their victims, as they would ask for an incredibly large ransom from the family of, say, a poor rural schoolteacher, who'd had a hard time even putting together the fare for the taxi from which he was violently abducted. It's become, quite simply, endemic.

Today the so-called 'bandits' are in the news almost daily, kidnapping anyone unfortunate enough to run into their ambushes. They might be seen as ragtag, but take a closer look at their activities, and one would see a dire pattern of organisation, much like some twisted form of a loose feudal structure. In other words, much like the organised crime families of the West, which have been romanticised by Hollywood for over half a century. They are mostly of Fulani ethnic stock, nomadic in nature and historically a peace-loving group. So how did things spiral downwards so swiftly and so destructively? The answer is simple: politics.

For more than a decade I have edited the Saturday edition of one of Nigeria's most influential newspapers, and I saw the fate of the Fulani unfold before me almost in real time. I took particular interest in chronicling their stories and how they have fitted in – or haven't – all over the country and beyond. Attacks on their camps and settlements, with their women and children killed and large herds of cattle rustled, gradually became regular events, buoyed by political language that had always harped on about their 'otherness'. With the volume of attacks, their value system was gradually eroded and arguably gave birth to what sensationalist newspapers call 'Fulani herdsmen' today.

Now, it took me a while to believe that Fulani people were responsible for marauding attacks on communities close to their settlements, sometimes reported as 'reprisal killings'. These 'reprisals' occurred across states such as Plateau, Taraba, Benue and, of course, Kaduna. But the mediation that should precede resolution and some sort of healing is almost always non-existent. Some of the disenfranchised rural Fulani retreated into the wilderness with whatever was left of their family and cattle. A peaceful, productive lifestyle would soon be replaced by something new, dark and, quite frankly, unhinged.

As mentioned earlier, a couple of years before my 2017 run-in with the 'bandits' I would often greet the news of a 'Fulani herder attack' with rolling eyes of disbelief, but a fateful evening encounter would violently change my position. That would bring us to the second of the two important markers of my life that I lost, which is the 'death' of Kaduna, two weeks after my father died, and I was there at home with family and friends. Earlier in the day I got a call from the office about an event outside Nigeria at which my boss suggested I represent him, with the excellent thought that it could help ease my mind of grief. I accepted, before learning the flight would depart from Lagos.

I drove in the company of my friend Umar to the Hamdala Hotel to buy a plane ticket, but it was late evening, and the office was closed. One thing left to do was to drive to the airport and secure a ticket against the next morning. That was fine, as I had to drop Umar off at the air force base where he lives anyway. The drive to the airport was uneventful, and I bought a ticket. As we drove back, I noticed it was getting darker, about 6.50 p.m. Umar and I chatted as we passed the Commandant's Gate of the Nigerian Defence Academy (which was attacked in August 2021 by 'bandits', who killed two military officers and kidnapped another). At that point Umar suggested I leave him at a major bus stop beside the base, as he wanted to visit a friend and didn't want to burden me. I refused, of course, and insisted that I drive him to his friend's, to which he reluctantly agreed. We reached the junction where a new road branches off the main highway, beside the College of Forestry (also later a target of the 'bandits' in a high-profile kidnapping of thirty-nine students in March 2021), leading to the new Rigasa train station. I drove into the road as a shortcut, without realising how big a mistake that was.

'What road is this?' Umar asked. 'Oh, a shortcut,' I offered, pointing out the brand-new asphalt and the fact that it was lined with solar-powered street lights. He countered with the observation that it was also very quiet. Remember, this was early days, before the massive boom in kidnapping and banditry close to the city. I shrugged it off and reassured him that I'd plied the road several times to pick up or drop off friends at the train station. It was about 7 p.m., and in the sky ribbons of purple and strings of orange were being overpowered by the dark, and fast. We drove on.

Ahead, by one of the solar lights, I saw a flashlight flickering up and down as if to flag us down. I slowed, assuming it was a

Nigeria is plagued by conflicts between nomadic herders and farmers – particularly in the centre and north and above all in Kaduna State. The violence moves along the routes taken by the livestock and has also reached the south-east. Desertification has deprived the herders, most of them Fulani, of the pastures where they have roamed for at least three hundred years, during which they established a Muslim aristocracy stretching as far as Kafanchan, a town to the south of Kaduna in the centre of the country. Now they are moving ever southwards, putting them into conflict with the farmers, most of them Hausa, who own the plots of land where their livestock is put out to pasture. But the area of unoccupied land is growing ever smaller and used by more and more animals, given that the Nigerian population has more than doubled over the past thirty years, as has the number of livestock. The government is trying to calm the disputes by setting aside land for the herders and giving them the opportunity to come together in larger communities, but not all Nigerian states are prepared to cooperate, and some, particularly further south, are refusing to hand over any land. The transition from a nomadic to a sedentary life is not always a happy one for the herders either – in fact, it can lead to a sense of isolation because, according to some Fulani, it removes the sense of community and collaboration that was created between them and the villages they used to visit. In the meantime, the transhumance routes are disappearing, amid privatisation and the construction of infrastructure. Those on either side of the dispute are now taking justice into their own hands, with kidnappings, killings and reprisals fuelled by the ready availability of weapons in the Sahel region following the Libyan crisis of 2011.

police checkpoint. But, as I eased off the accelerator, I also noticed there were six other figures, three on each side of the road. It was clear they weren't cops. Just as I voiced my misgivings to my friend, we suddenly heard a gunshot from behind. At this point, my spine froze and dozens of thoughts flooded my mind. Not sure what was behind us – and also not sure if we would survive a U-turn – I managed to gather myself together and accelerate ahead, putting the car's turbocharged engine to the test.

Within seconds we were face to face with the 'bandits' or potential kidnappers. Those on my side wore ill-fitting camouflage uniforms, rubber shoes that looked like crocs and had AK-47s slung over their shoulders. They also looked very, very Fulani. At high speed I drove towards their barricade, which, it appeared, was just being set up for the evening's business. I noticed a small gap on my side, next to which three of them stood, and I charged in that direction. Two fellows jumped into the ditch by the roadside. The other one was slow to leap, and my front bumper clipped his knee, sending him rolling over my bonnet, then windscreen, before landing violently on the floor.

As I drove over their crude barricade, the baddies on Umar's side opened fire. The bullets sprayed without precision, as AK-47s tend to do, especially since 'bandits' sometimes saw off their barrels. All I saw was gunfire blazing, and all I heard was the sound of possible death, prompting an adrenaline rush. My car, a trusty Peugeot, facilitated our escape and, damaged by the bullets, stopped by itself in a safe place, and I breathlessly called for a tow. The driver dropped Umar off, and I was taken home, where I quietly ate dinner, took a cold shower and retired to bed. I didn't sleep a wink, of course.

More than 525 languages are spoken in Nigeria, accounting for 7 per cent of all known languages. In addition to English, the official language, and Pidgin (also called Naija or Broken English), the largest are Hausa, Yoruba and Igbo, spoken by approximately 52, 42 and 34 million people respectively. Two other languages – Fula (or Fulani) and Efik-Ibibio – have more than 10 million speakers, and a number of others have between five and 10 million. There are also languages as yet unclassified and of uncertain origin.

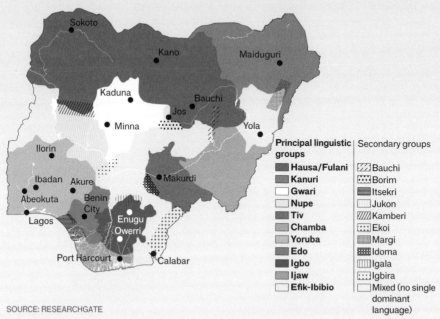

Principal linguistic groups

- Hausa/Fulani
- Kanuri
- Gwari
- Nupe
- Tiv
- Chamba
- Yoruba
- Edo
- Igbo
- Ijaw
- Efik-Ibibio

Secondary groups

- Bauchi
- Borim
- Itsekri
- Jukon
- Kamberi
- Ekoi
- Margi
- Idoma
- Igala
- Igbira
- Mixed (no single dominant language)

SOURCE: RESEARCHGATE

Ethnic make-up

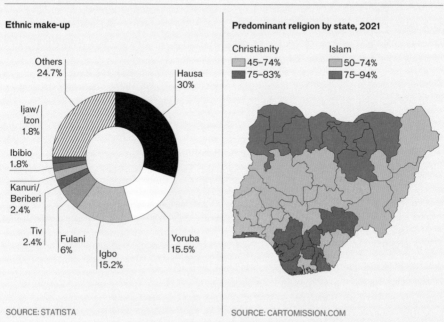

- Others 24.7%
- Hausa 30%
- Ijaw/Izon 1.8%
- Ibibio 1.8%
- Kanuri/Beriberi 2.4%
- Tiv 2.4%
- Fulani 6%
- Igbo 15.2%
- Yoruba 15.5%

SOURCE: STATISTA

Predominant religion by state, 2021

Christianity
- 45–74%
- 75–83%

Islam
- 50–74%
- 75–94%

SOURCE: CARTOMISSION.COM

I travelled to Lagos in the morning and came back a bit less frazzled. But that was when it dawned on me that my beloved Kaduna had 'died'.

By early 2019 the kidnappings – as ridiculous as it sounds – were becoming more frequent, brazen and increasingly mainstream. By then medium-to-large groups of brigands had formed or come to light and were occupying camps deep in the sparse, rocky wilderness of Zamfara State as well as the dense forests of Kaduna and Kano states. In Zamfara the modus operandi was primarily to stake a claim on rural communities and collect a form of 'protection money', which they refer to as 'taxes' in the local language. They would later begin to kidnap anyone they felt like, from young brides-to-be to elderly men and even women and children. They had no guiding code or political agenda, just raw, murderous criminality. And that was before the Boko Haram affiliations began.

Large-scale crime requires weapons and hardware, which the 'bandits' inexplicably own. Additionally, it requires training. And that's where the deadly insurgents who have been plaguing Nigeria for well over a decade come in. Boko Haram fighters fleeing the military onslaught in the north-east found home and industry among their forest-dwelling counterparts in other states. Actual interviews with 'bandits' have shown that there is indeed a strong link between the two groups of terrorists. One wants an Islamic state, and the other just wants money, cattle and power. As the kidnappings increased, so did the size of the ransoms. Initial demands can begin as high as 100 million naira (roughly $250,000) but would come down to as low as two million naira (about $4,000) after intense negotiations and haggling, much as cattle is traded in village markets.

Not all ransoms demanded are huge or are even for money, however. Sometimes the 'bandits' – especially those in rural areas – are so hard up that a teenage girl's ransom can be as low as a single chicken or a bag of rice. Recently, in Kaduna, the state government shut down telecommunications services to smoke the 'bandits' out. It seemed to do the trick briefly, because they became cut off from informal supply chains that brought food and other essentials to their forest hideouts. It became so dire for them that they began to ask for ransoms in the way of cooked food, specifically jollof rice or beef stew. While all that might seem comical in a twisted sense, it is not always so. Sometimes young girls are forcefully taken in 'marriage', impregnated and eventually sent back home to poor parents with a 'dowry', sometimes of as little as 15,000 naira (about $35).

In Kano State's dreaded Falgore Forest, the 'bandits' also operated freely – taking travellers, mostly poor farmers or rural traders and the occasional local politician – up to late 2019, when a large-scale military campaign flushed them out, fragmenting them into smaller groups that were forced to go deeper into the wilderness or join up with others. The forest currently serves as a training ground for the Nigerian Army, something that has brought relative peace to the area. However, that means a swelling in the ranks of other criminal gangs that occupy the forests of Kaduna and the hills that line the now-feared Kaduna–Abuja highway.

Kaduna State's 'bandit' problem is one of the worst. The once vibrant route that truckers took to Lagos, the Birnin Gwari highway, had always linked the northern part of Nigeria to the south-west, making economic activities easy, fast and convenient. But today the road is practically

deserted because of frequent raids on commercial buses, taxis and food-laden trailers. To drive along that highway as it is now is to face the risk of being kidnapped by the 'bandits' or, worse, death by the bullets they spray wantonly during their attacks. The area is particularly conducive to them because of the dense vegetation and vast forests of tall, leafy trees. That usually means the soldiers deployed to find and neutralise the 'bandits' and destroy their ramshackle camps have a hard time locating them. The air force has successfully bombed a number of camps over the years, but even that has yet to stop them, as more camps and groups spring up after one is destroyed, much like a nasty Hydra.

On the other side of Kaduna, on the way to the federal capital city of Abuja, 'bandits' are currently thriving despite the best efforts of security personnel – in particular the army but also joint task forces consisting of the army, air force and police. There are many and frequent patrols along the highway, which have proven insufficient, as the 'bandits' would strike quickly, kill commuters, kidnap people and vanish into the forests, sometimes going over the hills covered with lush vegetation to constantly shifting lairs. It is this kind of fluidity of movement that has angered fiery state governor

Above: A woman cooks lunch in Goska, a village in Kaduna State that was attacked in 2016 by a group of suspected herdsmen.
Opposite: Two men heading for the village of Kwaja, Adamawa State.

THE PASSENGER   Abdulkareem Baba Aminu

THE CHIBOK SCHOOLGIRLS

On 14 April 2014 a group of armed men burst into the dormitory of a girls' school in Chibok in the north-east. The men were militants belonging to Boko Haram, a violent jihadi group active in the region, which is opposed to female education (its Hausa name is often translated as 'Western education is forbidden'). They kidnapped 276 young women. The news spread around the world thanks to the hashtag #BringBackOurGirls posted alongside the names and photographs of the victims. A three-year saga of talks, releases, ransoms and escapes ensued, and quite a few of the girls were freed. Many of the survivors were offered international and national study programmes. Coming from a rural area where female education is often neglected, the Chibok girls were given opportunities that would previously have been unthinkable. This all came at an extremely high cost, however, because Boko Haram continued to hunt for them, and so the government had to protect them. More than a hundred girls enrolled in classes at the American University of Nigeria but were reduced to living incognito under guard, in clear contrast to the proclamations of liberation. Also, some activists claim the affair became a source of funds for the government given its high profile; after all, it is hardly the only case of young women being kidnapped in Nigeria. Eventually interest moved on from the wellbeing of the victims to a sensationalisation of the facts, which drives economic support for the fight against terrorism. Meanwhile many of the Chibok girls are still in captivity, and so the demonstrations calling for them all to be returned continue, albeit with ever dwindling numbers.

El-Rufai into saying in early 2022 that 'the only good bandit is a dead bandit'. His stance and statements reflect the kind of frustration felt by a number of reasonable Nigerian elected officials and traumatised citizens. As it is right now, his state seems to be surrounded by the kidnapping 'bandits' – with the outskirts and suburbs of towns and cities facing regular attacks and residents taken, especially between early 2019 and mid-2021.

The 'bandits' are part of the national zeitgeist, more than they have ever been. On 7 July 2021, my birthday, I was working, delivering a lecture to mid-level and senior journalists on 'Converging Media at the Dangote Academy' in faraway and scenic Obajana, a shortish drive from Kogi State's capital. While the participants and I had a most memorable experience, it almost wasn't the case. When I was informed it was to be held in Lokoja I declined because of the stories of abductions, armed robbery and even killings by the tragically misnamed 'bandits' on the road there. But, after some persuasion by colleagues, I agreed to give the lecture. Then a week

after that the news broke about an attack on the same road. I had probably escaped being a victim by a few hours. Time and chance, really.

Then take, for instance, the case of more than a hundred schoolchildren abducted from Tegina in Niger State in May 2021, after which they remained in captivity for three months before they were said to have been rescued by security forces. I can dare to imagine the heartbreak of the parents but not the abject terror and suffering the youngsters will have gone through. Rural communities in Niger State – which shares a border with Abuja – have for a long time been suffering in the grip of terrorists who kidnap, rape and kill at will. So when Governor Sani Bello assented to a new law that recommended death by hanging for kidnappers and cattle-rustlers in his state it was widely hailed. However, up to today, nothing has been heard about results.

In February 2021, in an incredible show of brazenness, Auwalun Daudawa, the now infamous leader of a gang terrorising Katsina State – incidentally President Muhammadu Buhari's home state – laid down his arms as part of an 'amnesty programme' introduced by the state government. This was after having shocked the nation by masterminding the abduction of more than three hundred schoolboys from a secondary school in December 2020. At the public event he said he led that attack because the state governor, Aminu Masari, vowed never to open a dialogue with them. 'Since [the government] said they were not interested in a peace deal, and they were sending military jets to torment our people and destroy what we had, we should take the battle to those who are not interested in peace,' he had said. However, not long after that – and to nobody's surprise – Daudawa returned to the forests and his criminal ways. Then in early May 2021, a mere nine days later, he was shot dead in a gunfight with soldiers as he attempted to rustle a large herd of cattle.

The 'bandits' of Katsina State have always been a weird lot. They rationalise their criminality, they even try to explain it away by blaming the government and by declaring their indifference to the author-ities. Mid-January 2022, and after a recent, slight shift from hardcore kidnapping, a group of bandits 'levied' operators at an artisanal gold mine at Jibia in the same state. A charge of 10,000 naira (about $20) was placed for 'uninterrupted utilisation' of the site. While that has not stopped the seventy-plus miners and processors who mine the site, the levy was placed after a violent attack days before left two miners dead and many injured. The police response was, as usual, half-hearted. The state's public relations officer, Superintendent of Police Gambo Isah, said, 'We've already launched an investiga-tion into the real motives of the bandits.' The short, uninformative and uninspiring response might as well have been any response from any police spokesman from any state in Nigeria.

More than half of Nigeria's thirty-six states are suffering a kidnapping 'bandit' problem, but perhaps the most shocking is when the criminals operate so close to the federal capital, Abuja. Wild theories even suggest that the criminals have put down deep roots in all the states that surround the capital city, with a variety of players that even include Boko Haram offshoots in Nasarawa and Kogi states. But, apart from media grandstanding and big-worded press releases, little or nothing is done, as kidnappings and killings continue to be reported so close to the nation's seat of power. Security operatives, including the army and air force, are overstretched and underequipped. However, according to insiders, recent changes in the leadership of the armed forces are seeing a marked change of pace in the engagement with the 'bandits'.

Even then 'banditry' continues to expand territory, much like an industry, while the rest of us are painted into a corner. That is why the government needs to think outside the proverbial box. The institutions responsible for our safety need to come together to secure our nation, as the incidents continue to heighten and worsen; if they are not adequately equipped, failure is almost certain, while the figurative cancer continues to spread. By the time we are all held captive, who will pay our collec-tive ransom? As I recollected earlier, after the trauma of losing my father to illness I almost lost my life to 'bandits', events that still replay in my head to this day. People say losing a parent hurts less with time, and the government has announced countless times that they will solve the 'bandit problem'. After more than five years it is clear they are all lying. ✒

THE NIGER DELTA

Abandoned boats on the riverbank
in Okrika, Port Harcourt.

Quite apart from its corrupting influence and economic and social impacts, the oil curse in Nigeria is also responsible for environmental devastation. Catastrophic damage has been caused to an ecosystem ranked third in the world for biodiversity, and the scourge of illegal refining is proving hard to root out, but the capital of the Niger Delta, Port Harcourt, is also a place of extraordinary resilience.

NOO SARO-WIWA

161

I'm in a canoe being punted by a fisherman who is standing up and digging his pole into the bed of the shallow river, pushing the boat forward. The Azumini River is a clear blue-green. Flanked by tall grasses and trees that rustle as a colobus monkey swings between the branches. A jacana bird with its orange and blue plumage swoops down to catch a fish.

I am in awe of my surroundings, having never seen such a pristine natural environment in this part of the world. But I have had to drive a couple of hours from my home town of Port Harcourt to come here and enjoy it. The Azumini River lies on the eastern edge of the Niger Delta, a huge river system that begins as a trickle in the uplands of the Guinea Highlands near the Sierra Leonean border, then arcs in a crescent through Mali before making a sharp turn south through Nigeria and splitting into several channels known as the Niger Delta on its approach towards the Atlantic.

The delta is the abundant life source for millions of people who have farmed and fished here for thousands of years. Yet today it is synonymous throughout the world as one of the most polluted places on the planet, thanks to its petroleum industry. Since 1956 the region's huge oil reserves have been extracted by multinational oil companies, including Agip, BP, Chevron and Shell. Oil has become vital to Nigeria's economy. Generations of mostly corrupt politicians have relied on it to the extent that it still accounts for 65 per cent of federal revenue as the economy remains undiversified.

Meanwhile, the natural environment has paid the price. Left to its own devices, nature in the Niger Delta is fiercely abundant. Towering iroko hardwood trees and palm trees overlook the world's third most biodiverse ecosystem. Mangroves line the innumerable waterways, nursing countless fish species. But all this flora and fauna has been catastrophically damaged, partly by countless oil spills and pollution.

I was born in the delta's biggest city, Port Harcourt, in the 1970s. Back then it was known as the 'Garden City' – and for good reason. I can still remember the road medians with potted plants on them, and trees sprouted everywhere – there was even a forest next door to our house. But urbanisation and concrete have taken over. Nigeria's unemployment rate is said to be 30 per cent, but that's just the official figure. In reality, everyone is hustling to make a living. The roadsides are filled with women selling fruit and vegetables. Men cart mountains of carrots in wheelbarrows. Ethnic Hausa currency exchangers in their white Islamic robes sit on the roadside offering their services to foreign-looking types like myself. A man with a limp carries a crate of potatoes on his head without dropping them, miraculously. Traffic vendors sell watches, brooms, remote controls. Nature must take a back

NOO SARO-WIWA is a writer and journalist and is the daughter of Ken Saro-Wiwa, the Nigerian writer and environmental activist executed for taking a stance against the oil multinationals. She grew up in the UK, studied at Columbia University, New York, and now lives in London. In 2012 she published her debut, *Looking for Transwonderland: In Search of Nigeria* (Soft Skull, USA / Granta, UK, 2012), which was *The Sunday Times* travel book of the year and was described by the *Guardian* as one of the ten best books ever written about Nigeria. Her second book, *Black Ghosts*, to be published by Canongate in 2023, is a journey through the African community in China.

'An investigative journalist once told me he once witnessed a uniformed army colonel salute deferentially to a powerful, denim-clad oil-bunkerer.'

seat to this hustle. Once upon a time you could smell the tropical vegetation in the thick, humid air. Now it is petrol fumes and – even worse – soot. The black stuff tumbling from the sky is now one of Port Harcourt's most defining characteristics. It is a side effect of the illegal oil refining, or 'artisanal refining'. Poverty has made oil so expensive for ordinary Nigerians that people began stealing it from pipelines and refining it themselves. Nobody knows exactly how they learned this skill. In any case, it is pretty ingenious, and, ironically, it demonstrates our capacity for innovation. But artisanal refining is a dangerous activity. It is male-dominated, macho work, carried out in the dead of night away from the authorities' eyes. Refiners get burned from explosions and carry the horrific scars on their skin. The guys at the bottom of the hierarchy make about 150,000 naira ($340) per month, an above-average wage. The top guys can make a staggering thirty million naira ($68,000) per day after expenses. So lucrative is the business that some corrupt politicians and military officials turn a blind eye in exchange for a slice of the profits. In this klepto-plutocracy the usual hierarchies are turned upside down: Patrick Naagbaton, the late investigative journalist, told me he once witnessed a uniformed army colonel salute deferentially to a powerful, denim-clad oil-bunkerer.

The artisanal refining sends particles into the air, which rain down on the city regularly. The soot gets on people's

hands, up their nostrils; it settles on their laundry on washing lines and even blocks out the sunlight in some areas. Residents complain endlessly about it. 'I'm constantly cleaning my apartment,' says Ese Emerhi, a Port Harcourt resident. 'First thing in the morning, again in the afternoon and again in the evening. The soot just covers everywhere. I never open my windows to get fresh air. I can't do that. We are breathing this every day, every night. I don't want to think about what it's doing to our internal organs. Ten years from now there will be a health crisis. Babies growing up with asthma and coughs.'

Were my father, Ken Saro-Wiwa, still alive he would be complaining vociferously about this problem. He had long campaigned against the oil industry damaging the Niger Delta's fragile and valuable ecosystem. In the early 1990s he started a campaign to fight against environmental damage by Shell in the land of our ethnic group, the Ogoni. The threat my father posed to the military dictatorship was so great that he and eight of his colleagues were eventually arrested on trumped-up charges and sentenced to death following a kangaroo-court trial in 1995. They were killed on 10 November that year.

My father's death left a legacy of political agitation, which evolved into militant action by jobless and frustrated young men, particularly from the Ijaw ethnic group. They sabotaged oil pipelines (cutting Nigeria's production by as much

Born in 1941 in Ogoni territory in the Niger Delta, Ken Saro-Wiwa was a writer and political activist. After graduating from university and a brief career as a teacher, in 1985 he made his literary debut with the novel *Sozaboy*. Subtitled *A Novel in Rotten English*, the 'rotten English' in question was a mixture of standard British English and Nigerian Pidgin expressions; post-colonial studies still uses the term rotten English when discussing writers who use local languages that developed during colonial times. In 1990, by that point an established writer and with highly successful television programmes to his name, he joined the Movement for the Survival of the Ogoni People (MOSOP), a non-violent group that fought for the rights of the Ogoni, who live in a region extremely rich in oil but where most local people saw none of the benefits of its extraction, which instead went to big foreign concerns (notably Shell) and a minority of the population. The environmental damage, however, affected everyone, especially those who lived off the land. MOSOP organised peaceful marches attracting up to 300,000 people, which were repressed by the complicit Nigerian regime. The writer was arrested multiple times and finally sentenced to death following a show trial, and Saro-Wiwa was hanged in November 1995 while a scandalised international community looked on. Shell was subsequently accused of being implicated in Saro-Wiwa's death and the violence used against activists, but the company denied any involvement – yet in 2009 it agreed to pay compensation to the victims totalling $15.5 million.

as one-third in some years) and began kidnapping oil workers to extract money from the oil companies. In 2009 the Nigerian government offered an amnesty to these militants in exchange for a cessation of violence. It also paid each of them a monthly stipend of 65,000 naira ($145 at today's rate). But a culture of lawlessness remained, and the kidnappings became less about politics and more about making money. The abductors turned towards their fellow penniless citizens. Nowadays, even the women who sell potatoes on the roadside are abduction targets.

'The real kidnappers from the old days were very intelligent,' says Suanu, a former militant, with whom I'm chatting in a café in Bori, the town where my father was born. Suanu gave up his violent life and now preaches peace to the youth. 'The kidnappers used to do their research. They picked their targets carefully,' he laments.

It's a sad state of affairs when former militants feel morally superior to the current crop.

The region's high levels of insecurity have turned the oil companies' residential areas into fortresses. Oil workers and their families wanting to leave the compound can only go to 'approved' locations in Port Harcourt. I often see them sunbathing by the pool in the Novotel hotel where security guards check all incoming cars with metal detectors. And in the skies overhead small jets and helicopters fly over the hotel from a nearby airfield, transporting oil workers to installations in the delta.

Opposite top: A dead fish pond in Rivers State, which remains polluted following an oil spill that occurred in 2009.
Opposite bottom: An oil slick on the river at Bodo, Rivers State.

Oil spills by company, 2010–22

It is estimated that over the past 50 years between 10 and 13 million tonnes of oil has been released into the environment, of which 77 per cent has not been recovered. Spills are caused by sabotage, exploration-related activities, oil-plant breakdowns, pipeline corrosion and tanker accidents.

● Shell   ● ENI   ● Chevron   ○ Others

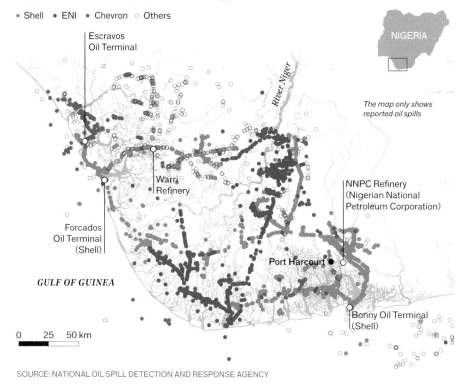

Escravos
Oil Terminal

NIGERIA

River Niger

*The map only shows
reported oil spills*

Warri
Refinery

NNPC Refinery
(Nigerian National
Petroleum Corporation)

Forcados
Oil Terminal
(Shell)

GULF OF GUINEA

Port Harcourt ●

Bonny Oil Terminal
(Shell)

0   25   50 km

SOURCE: NATIONAL OIL SPILL DETECTION AND RESPONSE AGENCY

Shell has a recreation club, which my siblings and I used to frequent when we were young, in the years before my father started his campaign against the company. It was the only place where we could play tennis or swim in an outdoor pool. It had been a long time since I'd been there, but I get a chance to revisit it through an acquaintance, Eloise (not her real name), who works at one of the European embassies. Eloise lives in the residential area for French oil company Total, which lies adjacent to Shell's residential area. She invites me to check both of them out.

After I pass through the security gates, Eloise lends me one of her bicycles, and we cycle in the dying sunset through the Total compound. It is one of the few places one can cycle in Port Harcourt, where the roads are full of heavy, no-lane traffic and open ditches. I revel in the freedom of being able to cycle freely and enjoy the cool breeze on my face. Eloise and I cycle past neat houses along tree-lined, tarmacked roads that are mostly devoid of traffic.

There are recycling bins, in contrast to the garbage that carpets Port Harcourt's streets. People whizz past us on roller skates and bicycles, greeting Eloise. So much tranquillity.

The Shell compound is much bigger than Total's, with taller, older trees and a central park and a nine-hole golf course illuminated by floodlights that buzz with insects and make lovely silhouettes of the trees. The greenery is a refreshing contrast to the concrete torpor of the rest of the city. How ironic that the oil company that helped wreck our environment should create such a green and clean-aired oasis for itself.

Shell's and Total's residential areas are another universe. But Port Harcourt is a city of enclaves; people barricading themselves and creating paradises within their four walls. One such place, and one of my favourite houses on earth, is the home of artist Diseye Tantua. Known for his Afro Pop Art paintings that combine symbols, bright colours and text expressing traditional proverbs, Tantua's home in the west of the city is a living embodiment of his work. The entire house is a playful wonderland of dazzlingly bright colours, stained-glass windows, sculptures, paintings and framed posters. Almost every inch of the walls is covered in paintings purchased from other artists, many of which allude to popular street images and proverbs found on Nigeria's vehicles. Car parts are repurposed into furniture. A Mercedes grille and headlights form the end of a bed. There's a Volkswagen seat and grille by a doorway. In the kitchen his wife, who runs a bakery business, is blowtorching the sugar on pots of crème brûlée. She prepares us garri and okra soup, which we eat by the upper balcony carpeted in green turf that contrasts boldly with the house's purple exterior.

CURSED RESOURCES

The history of Nigeria is closely entwined with the extraction of oil from the Niger Delta, which began in 1957, shortly before independence, and is an exemplary case of the so-called 'resource curse', the paradox by which countries with abundant natural resources tend to develop more slowly. Oil receipts strengthen the currency, making other sectors less competitive, the national budget depends on the oscillations of oil prices, the failure to redistribute the proceeds ignites ethnic and regional tensions and the vast financial flows are concentrated in the hands of the few – the army, in the case of Nigeria – weakening institutions and fuelling corruption and bad government. The nationalisation of the oil sector in 1971, which forced the multinationals into joint ventures with the state-owned NNPC, enriched a minuscule fraction of the population and did nothing to stop the environmental devastation that has transformed the delta into one of the most polluted places on the planet. Today the spills are mainly caused by minor thefts and acts of sabotage, but the most disastrous documented incidents were the responsibility of the oil majors – Shell above all, but also Chevron, Exxon and ENI – whose efforts to clean up were decidedly unsatisfactory. With cases under way in Nigerian and international courts and with the costs linked to theft and sabotage, the majors are starting to think their operations are no longer worth the trouble. In 2021 Shell, in the fortunate position of being able to wash its hands of the sooty mess, announced it wanted to sell its offshore installations.

On the ground level I see a dog sculpture by the internationally renowned artist Dotun Popoola, who creates effigies out of scrap metal. Near the dog is an amazing peacock made out of spoons plus a large bust of Bob Marley fashioned from metal chains. I sit on a bench created from a pink Mercedes boot lid, with the side doors attached perpendicularly to form 'armrests'. Inside, the bar is comprised of the yellow boot lid of a Lagos taxi. It is here that Diseye regularly entertains music and poetry salons, where musicians and artists gather to drink and inspire one another. Events such as these mainly take place within the home for safety reasons. People in this city tend not to stay outdoors after 8 or 9 p.m. Diseye's house is a glorious break from the city and its economic decline and the diminishing cultural life that flows from that.

'Port Harcourt is finished,' one guest tells me. The recent phase of decline started in 2017, due partly to the recession caused by a drop in the price of crude oil. The guest owns a new BMW but says if he ever had to drive it around at night he wouldn't dare stop for fear of robbers and kidnappers. Not even at traffic lights. 'I'll crush anything that moves,' he says bluntly. One would expect an artist like Diseye to have moved to Lagos, Nigeria's biggest city and cultural capital, but he stays in Port Harcourt because of his wife's business and daughter Chloe's schooling. Port Harcourt is all the better for it.

One week I travel out of Port Harcourt to see the oil spills and other environmental damage for myself. The first place I visit is the town of Bodo, thirty kilometres south-east of Port Harcourt and scene of one of the worst oil spills in recent history. In 2008 two leakages released more than 500,000 barrels of petroleum on to the community's land. On the morning of the spill it had been raining, and people woke up to fat, black droplets of oil plopping from the sky. The inundation destroyed around 1,000 hectares of mangroves and all its marine life, which the Bodo people relied on for their livelihood as fishermen and farmers. The community sued Shell, and in 2015 the multinational company accepted liability for the spills, agreeing to pay $83 million to Bodo villagers and to clean up their lands and waterways.

The oil, however, is still there, albeit not as thick as before. They've cleared the top part of the slick, so the water is a little clearer, but everything is still caked in

Right: The artist and collector Diseye Tantua in Port Harcourt, Rivers State, and (**opposite page**) one of his creations, a bed constructed from an old Mercedes-Benz.

black, and the vegetation is dead. A large tree has fallen, its trunk black and lifeless. The sight of a few dead, stubby mangrove roots was depressing. This once green and blue, lush landscape was leached of all its colour. Everything appeared grey or black.

I pulled up by the waterside and met a resident named Michael. He works as a surveillance officer but was a fisherman as a child. He tells us that the fishermen now have to travel some way downriver to catch fish in unreserved waters. As the Bodo mangroves have died, some of their boys steal mangrove branches from other towns further downstream to use as fuel. Michael is one of many residents who received 600,000 naira ($1,350) compensation from Shell. They have used the money to build new homes, hence the relative smartness of certain sections of Bodo, but the town still lacks infrastructure like electricity and water. They have to drink the dirty local water. Michael's house may look good, but it is very close to the oil slick. In another universe it might have been a sought-after home in a prime residential location, with 'picturesque' views of the water.

One legacy of my father's campaign and death is that the UN conducted a formal assessment of the environmental damage caused by the oil industry. The UN found huge amounts of carcinogens in the soil and water and ordered the Nigerian federal government to fund a $1 billion clean-up. The Hydrocarbon Pollution Remediation Project (HYPREP) was subsequently launched to carry it out, but locals say little has been done in the past few years. Suspicions of corruption run high. The promises of jobs for Ogoni youths in the clean-up process haven't materialised. In K-Dere district I drive past the hollow carcass of a HYPREP vehicle burned out by frustrated Ogoni youths. HYPREP says it can't employ many of them because they lack the necessary skills.

So the temptation to make money

through illegal refining continues. In a small house in Bodo I meet a young artisanal refiner named Barizondu (meaning 'God Will Come'). He is wearing a black shirt, black trousers and a red bow tie; probably his church outfit – it's a Sunday afternoon. He looks about seventeen but is actually twenty-seven years old and has a girlfriend and small child. Barizondu has worked in illegal refining since 2014. Of his eight siblings he is the only one with the semblance of an education. Barizondu tells me he can earn up to 100,000 naira ($225) a week but as little as 15,000 naira ($35). Sometimes he goes without work for up to three months when the federal government launches one of its occasional crackdowns. He doesn't invest his money, however, and has few savings. He wants to get out of the business because 'it's risky', but he is able to help his grandmother financially, so there's some satisfaction from that. She is pleased at the money she receives – as a farmer she can no longer grow crops because the soil is too polluted. If Barizondu knows the irony of this vicious circle, he doesn't show it.

Among certain communities there's a nonchalance – or resignation perhaps – around the environmental dangers as people become used to it. And they are used to it – they simply need to get on with the business of everyday survival. Near the city of Warri, I visited one of the numerous gas flares – huge eight-metre flames in which hydrocarbons (a by-product of oil extraction) are burned off into the atmosphere. Up close, the noise is loud, like a NASA rocket launch. These days the oil companies, mindful of the world's disapproving eyes, nestle these gas flares in vegetation and point them at a 90-degree angle to limit their visibility from a distance.

But the sideways positioning of the

CROSS RIVER

While oil extraction has devastated the Niger Delta, the nearby state of Cross River, in the far southeast of the country, is known for its natural parks and is home to half of the country's rainforests. According to a (far from reliable!) 2018 study, two of the country's four most visited destinations were resorts in Cross River. One is a luxury operation, Obodu Mountain, a cattle ranch set in the verdant mountains on the border with Cameroon, but the other is somewhat more controversial. The Tinapa Business Resort, a few kilometres from the regional capital Calabar, is a vast project worth over $350 million that was initiated by Donald Duke, the respected governor of the state between 1999 and 2007. It includes retail spaces, casinos, cinemas and film studios, restaurants, discotheques, an artificial lake and more besides. The business projections forecast three million visitors a year, but this was not realistic, partly because a dispute between the federal and state governments meant that the site could not offer a tax-free zone as promised and ultimately ended up with prices higher than average. Many accounts describe it as run down, so it is surprising to find it at the top of the most visited destinations ... There is no doubt that Cross River has a good reputation, however, and the local Efik population are proud of the cult of cleanliness and order that they believe makes their territory so welcoming.

'The delta could be saved if only the old-guard leadership would clear the way for the next generation. Everywhere I go I meet individuals who are smart and have ideas and energy and the passion to change things for the better.'

flames means the people of the Erue-mukohwarien community can now use the fire to dry the kpokpo cassava they cultivate. Men, women and children get incredibly close to the flame as they place their cassava on bamboo trays just a few metres away from this giant fireball. There's no steel fencing around the flare, only a meagre 1.2-metre-high wall of sandbags. The villagers climb over the bags and move shockingly close. They seem inured to the 150-degrees-Celsius heat. I'm standing just beyond the sandbags, yet my skin is singed and my eyes are watering painfully. The heat disables my phone temporarily. The signposts warning everyone to keep away are fading and written in poorly spelled English. One feels a distinct lack of government protection. Nobody is helping these villagers find an alternative source of income. For two days after visiting the flare my eyes are still watering, and I feel slightly ill.

After witnessing such scenes, I mourned the lost paradise that was the Niger Delta. Speak to the elders, and they will tell you about the crocodiles and alligators in the saltwater delta creeks in the 1970s. We had large pythons, bush pigs, tortoises, saltwater turtles, pygmy hippopotami, monkeys, chimpanzees and gorillas. A few remain in small numbers while others are extinct. It's hard to believe all this existed within my lifetime. When an elephant was spotted in Andoni it was reported in the news, such is the rarity of these animals.

A small portion of this pristine Niger Delta environment still exists in the Finima Nature Park in Bonny, an island right by the Atlantic Ocean. Here, in a 1,000-hectare parcel of land, one can experience a bit of the old, beautiful delta. Here tall trees tower over a forest containing ferns and the African grey parrot and other birds. I take a brief boat ride around its small lake. The surface of the water sparkles between the water lilies, and I can spot colourful birds among the trees.

The delta could be saved if only the old-guard leadership would clear the way for the next generation. Everywhere I go I meet individuals who are smart and have ideas and energy and the passion to change things for the better, but their efforts don't translate into a system-wide improvement for society because there are so many barriers preventing them from rolling out these ideas and monetising them.

At the southern end of Port Harcourt the river slows and divides into creeks that meander around islands. On the approach to Okrika, a creekside neighbourhood, the tarred road peters out. Housing developers never built up this part of town because it is prone to flooding. The area attracted poorer residents, who constructed shanty homes along the swampy waterfront. During the rainy season the water levels rise and combine with the poor sanitation to make Okrika a no-go area. Rightly or wrongly, the neighbourhood has a reputation for crime, and most city dwellers – police included – generally give it a wide

Above: Ese Emerhi, owner of the Marley & Blue café in Port Harcourt, with a customer.
Below: A sound engineer monitors a recording session at the Chicoco Radio studios in Port Harcourt.

berth. But in the previous decade the state government has tried to evict its half a million residents and build high-end developments.

The Okrika residents resisted eviction and, with the help of a non-governmental organisation, run a radio station called Chicoco Radio, which gives the community a platform. A group of young journalists have received professional training from Victoria Uwemedimo, a graduate of Columbia University Journalism School, who has roots in the Niger Delta. She returned here to help the Okrika people develop a voice and bring their marginalised community to life through radio stories. Their reporting on Okrika is more informative and entertaining than anything produced in the 'proper' media. They give insights into topics ranging from sex workers struggling to make a living to the notoriously zealous Special Anti-Robbery Squad police arresting people for tinting their hair. Chicoco also produces plays because, as one of its journalists puts it, 'Not everyone can read or likes music. But they might like drama.'

Chicoco fills the gap created by our authorities. Faith in government is thin in Port Harcourt. There's a 'lack of leadership', says Ese Emerhi, an international development worker. She is one of many people in the city who have taken matters into their own hands and created their own slice of paradise there. Her café in the Government Residential Area, Marley & Blue, is arguably Port Harcourt's best. It is a breath of fresh air – white walls, big windows that let in the light. I love the fact that Miles Davis plays low in the background rather than the usual thumping contemporary Nigerian music. The absence of loud music is a novelty in this country with its young population, where loud music blares out incessantly in every restaurant, café and shop. Peaceful spaces aren't easy to find.

Ese's first-time customers often don't know what to make of her café. 'They're not used to a space where there's no loud music, where there's no TV and they just have to sit there in a zen space ... It throws them off.' But they have grown to love that vibe.

Ese is determined to bring coffee culture to Port Harcourt and educate people about the beverage. 'Nigeria grows pretty decent coffee, it's just that nobody knows that we do.' We grow it in the north, a sweeter type of Arabica bean. The coffees at Marley & Blue are a blend of Ethiopian and Nigerian beans.

'Port Harcourt has the potential to be such an amazing space ... I hope this place can truly become a destination, just like Lagos or Abuja or even Kano.'

Ese, who grew up partly in England and partly in Port Harcourt, could live anywhere she pleases in Nigeria or Africa. Her job is a work-from-home one, so she doesn't have to be based here, but she is drawn to this city.

'PH folks have this "grit" about them that makes them do the impossible. It's not quite resilience, though there's that, too. But this grit is in the way we walk, how we enter a room, the dirty humour, the toughness. You might want to think twice about crossing someone from Port Harcourt because our madness has no bounds. And it is this love-hate relationship that I have with Port Harcourt that keeps me here. This place frustrates me daily, but it's also found me.' 🐦

Afrobeats: The Heartbeat of Nigeria

The Nigerian music industry is going through a real boom thanks to the high profile of Afrobeats internationally. This music is conquering the world, bolstering the country's soft power and filling Nigerians – both at home and in the diaspora – with pride. But where does the music come from and how does it tell the stories and soundtrack the collective struggles of Nigeria's people?

JOEY AKAN

Nigerian rapper Phyno performs at a show in Abuja organised by the popular singer Patoranking.

It's a humid night in Lagos, as young men and women pile at the gate of the Amore Gardens in Lekki, a swanky suburb of the city. It's a mixed crowd, local revellers jostling for access alongside diaspora returnees back in the country for the rush of the annual Lagos holiday party and concert circuit. Everyone is out for a good time. Nigerian pop artist Oxlade is celebrating a successful year with an all-star concert, and his fans have come from far and near to join in the happiness. You can hear the hype man compete with the DJ. 'Put your hands up if you're here for Oxlade,' he demands. Through the sea of answering hands raised high in the sky, the DJ cues in a new hit. The hands drop, the waists move, the bodies rock to the rhythm and everyone soaks in the high energy of the moment.

It's so good to be alive in Lagos right now. Just down the street another concert is in sway, this time hosted by another pop artist, L.A.X. The scene isn't much different from Amore Gardens. Gyrating bodies, loud music and the thick scent of sweat mixed with an occasional 'That's my jam!' The door at both ends stays revolving as attendees walk the three-minute distance between shows and performances, trying to maximise their enjoyment. Eating their cake and having it. And if you leave Lekki and take a drive into the upmarket neighbourhoods of Victoria Island, nearly every street has a party in swing. This is Lagos in December. This is the home of Afrobeats, where local artists make music in home studios and rake in enough numbers to compete with global pop stars.

2021 was an unprecedented year for African pop music. The Nigeria-led movement – long-time leaders on the continent – cracked the global pop framework. They're funnelling new music, a dynamic raft of artists and a rich cultural heritage into the world's mainstream consciousness. Singer Wizkid's 'Essence' – an R&B fusion collaboration with Tems, which later added Justin Bieber to the guest list – cracked the US Billboard Hot 100 chart on its way to becoming the global song of the summer. His compatriot CKay made an appearance in the same chart, while adding the distinction of being the most Shazamed song on the planet. CKay's TikTok-boosted hit, 'Love Nwantiniti', earned platinum certification after selling a million copies and single-equivalent sales in the USA. The record sits on top of an increasingly recognised conveyor belt of hits originating in Lagos. Nigerians have never experienced this level of success. It isn't what the music enthusiasts and professionals in the country are used to. And it's all happening so fast. The mood in Lagos is pure elation. Pop-culture

JOEY AKAN is a journalist, podcaster and commentator on music and pop culture. He lives in Lagos where he edits *Afrobeats Intelligence*, a weekly newsletter on African music.

history is happening right in front of us. And we are participants.

Nigeria is having a banner moment in world music, and the benefits are everywhere. The people are prouder. In major cities across the world Nigerian immigrants who make up the diaspora community now hold their heads higher. They're the new cool.

In the past six years the musical terrain of Lagos has changed. A casual drive around Victoria Island, Lekki and Ikoyi will take you past the local offices and partners of the largest music companies. The major record labels – Sony Music, Universal Music Group and Warner Music Group – all have offices in the city; distribution houses, including TuneCore, DistroKid, EMPIRE, Platoon and others, have put boots on the ground, setting up legal entities to do business in the creative industry. Every major company looking for a local partnership comes with funds, structure and expertise.

The aim is simple. Africa is the next frontier for global sounds, and Nigeria leads the charts with dynamic music, a large ubiquitous diaspora and energy that enlivens dance floors from Berlin to Oman. Global music corporations are swooping in to get in on the promise of world domination, build market share, extract the best cultural products and export them into spaces where they have the potential to influence new markets. The endgame is more money from everyone. The companies want it, the artists dream of it. It's the perfect marriage. 'Following the global success of a number of Afrobeats/Afro pop artists, the world has its eyes on Africa, and we keep churning out quality material and breaking boundaries. We have international labels backing our local labels/artists, and this has helped increase the reach of our music to the world. Also

REPATS

There are no official statistics covering the movement of emigrants who return to Nigeria after one or two generations in the West, yet their numbers are significant, to judge from their contribution to the economic and cultural scene in Lagos, and some estimates suggest ten thousand people a year. Known as 'repats', they constitute a pan-African phenomenon, where citizens who have been living outside the continent return to their ancestral homelands to reconnect with their culture. This often leads to disappointment, however, because these countries today are globalised developing nations, certainly not the timeless Edens they were when their families first left. Nigerian repats, however, are well aware of this; most of them were born in Nigeria or are from families that have only recently emigrated. What attracts these cultivated and well-educated citizens to a city like Lagos – a gigantic and ever-expanding metropolis with a middle class that is every bit as consumerist as anyone anywhere – are the career opportunities available to those with a degree, an entrepreneurial spirit and contacts within the global Nigerian diaspora. They open shops and found start-ups, work in television or import luxury goods, businesses that are over-represented in the Western countries they have left behind. But those who have made their return warn that while the opportunities are manifold so are the obstacles, and, if you are not prepared, jumping on the first plane back home is no guarantee of success.

'You can trace today's expansive international progress to Afrobeat's creator Fela Kuti. Arguably the most significant Nigerian musician to date, the inventive, anti-establishment performer shaped the identity of music in the country.'

our sound is different and beautiful,' says Isioma N, head of promotions at the Nigerian record label Chocolate City and the new player, Warner Music.

And it's all thanks to the internet. Once, a long time ago in the late 1990s and early 2000s, Nigerian music was different. American and British pop stars had local radio in a chokehold. Today's millennials grew up singing along to Westlife and Backstreet Boys, Missy Elliot and Jay-Z. Local pop music was largely non-existent and, if you found it, it would be crude imitations of their foreign counterparts. But young local creatives across multiple states began to experiment with local independent music to combat the dominance of American and British pop, reggae and hip-hop artists, mixing local flavour with foreign influences to achieve a balance. The music lacked a central, cohesive, signature sound, but everyone did what they could. And a few took off. Like the legend 2face Idibia, who mixed reggae and R&B to mad effect, scoring the global hit 'African Queen' in 2004. Like twin duo Psquare, who continue to pack stadiums with a variety of genres and a string of hits after two decades at the top of African music. And D'banj, who made the UK sit up and listen in 2012 after his smash hit 'Oliver Twist' pushed him and the sound into foreign waters. Everyone has had a role to play, but the road has been a long one.

The nature of creativity has never changed. Local pop music is dependent on extensive research and development and the fusion of new sounds. Nigeria is blessed with a plethora of roots sounds drawn from its heterogeneous cultures and maintained over generations through recording and release and distribution. There's highlife and ogene music in the east, apala and fuji from the west, the south produces a large number of genres reliant on local instruments and the north is replete with Arabic influences. It's a lot to work with. Local pop producers pick and choose from this sonic assortment, using it as an anchor. To achieve a truly new product they fuse these home-grown sounds with borrowed samples from other regions. This process hasn't changed for generations, despite advances in technology, but the final product is always in flux, like a living, breathing entity. While the music made in the early pop days of the late 1990s and early 2000s sounded a lot like their external influences from the USA and the Caribbean, local artists have continued to innovate, bringing the world closer with their productions. Wizkid's 2021 summer banger 'Essence' is processed in the USA as R&B. Never mind that the artist is Nigerian and the lyrics are delivered in Nigerian Pidgin English, the world connects with it. And people love it.

You can trace today's expansive international progress to Afrobeat's creator Fela Kuti. Arguably the most significant Nigerian musician to date, the inventive, anti-establishment performer shaped the

Reading Chimamanda Ngozi Adichie's *Purple Hibiscus* in 2005, Eghosa Imasuen, at the time an aspiring writer and later the founder of the publishing house Narrative Landscapes, had an epiphany: 'I knew those characters ... It was as if my generation had been given permission to speak ... And there's an audience for it.' The book was published by Farafina, at the time the only Nigerian publisher devoted to experimental writing, and Adichie was beginning to develop a prestigious reputation. Being published by a foreign publisher, however, was the only way to gain a pedigree as an author in the eyes of Nigerian readers in a country where the book market struggles to take off, partly because piracy erodes more than 70 per cent of earnings, and a book that sells five thousand copies is considered a bestseller. And yet something changed. Farafina was joined by Cassava Republic (established in 2006) and more recently OkadaBooks, which sells books to read on your smartphone. Port Harcourt was UNESCO's World Book Capital in 2014, and the Aké Festival, established in 2013 in Abeokuta, promotes and attracts writers from all over Africa in huge numbers. More and more Nigerian writers are becoming known outside the country, and the readership is growing as well, although the pandemic led to a crisis in the sector. And while it remains true that opting for a foreign publisher bestows a certain prestige, some writers instead choose dynamic, creative, home-grown publishers, just as Imasuen, who is now Adichie's publisher in Nigeria, had hoped. And finally, rather than Nigerian publishers just buying rights, Cassava Republic opened an office in London to sell rights to works by Nigerian authors to the rest of the world. Nigeria is no longer just a country of writers but also of publishers.

identity of music in the country. A journeyman with extensive influences from around the world, Fela Kuti found an inventive way to fuse American jazz, funk, drums and Yoruba chants to birth a new genre. But what he did with the influence of the music set him apart for ever.

The well-travelled son of a Nigerian women's rights activist, Funmilayo Ransome-Kuti, Fela and his band Africa '70 (featuring drummer Tony Allen) became stars in Nigeria during the 1970s. Backed by celebrity and a successful art form, he morphed into an outspoken critic and target of Nigeria's military juntas. In 1970 Fela founded the Kalakuta Republic commune, attracting a motley crowd of societal outliers, anti-establishment hippies and music enthusiasts. He later declared the commune independent from military rule, attracting the rage of the military regime. In 1978 the commune was destroyed in a raid. By 1984 Fela was in jail, condemned and convicted on a charge of currency smuggling by the military government of Muhammadu Buhari (who is, at the time of writing, the democratically elected president of Nigeria). After a twenty-month incarceration Fela continued to record and perform through the 1980s and into the 1990s. Since his death in 1997 his son Femi Kuti has kept his original works alive through reissues and compilations of his music.

Music is endemic to Nigeria. It is in every facet of our lives. Beyond parties, celebrations and personal journeys into escapism, Nigeria is a musical country. Mothers coax their kids to eat with a song. Bus conductors add melodies to the names of stops. Hawkers create inventive tunes to market their wares. Sound and melodies are encoded into every sliver of our collective being. Societies store their histories within folk tales and pass

'It's understood that the music won't heal us or usher in better days. Afrobeats will never make the pain go away, but it can make you feel good for a while.'

them down orally through generations to preserve culture. In religious worship, our traditional religions conduct rituals with specially designed songs to invoke the ancestors and alter elements for a favourable outcome. It's a part of us.

With Fela, Nigerians learned to utilise music for more than escapism and storytelling. Ailed by bad governance, economic instability and corruption, 1980s Nigeria was on the edge. As Fela railed against the machine, Afrobeat became a protest genre embodying the sighs of the oppressed, the cries of the hurting masses and an anchor for social justice demonstrations.

Today's dominant Afrobeats (don't forget the 's') can scarcely claim to be a descendant of Fela's creation. It is radically different. Although Nigeria's problems have remained consistent since the days of Fela, the protest music has dried up. Its world-beating substitute contains anti-establishment sentiments only in traces. Protest isn't cool in pop culture. The new generation of performers and patrons and audiences have designated music for something else: escapism.

With a population of around 200 million, Nigeria is currently the world's capital of poverty. According to a 2020 report by the Nigerian National Bureau of Statistics, 40 per cent of Nigerians (eighty-three million) live in poverty. Inflation continues to rise, alongside insecurity, the scourge of Boko Haram terrorists and marauding bandits in the north (see 'Abduction Nation' on page 149). Once again citizens are on the edge.

But the music isn't. It's a vacation. When the speakers come on and the drinks flow, on dancefloors, at parties and on street corners the mood is primarily one of escapism. People go to the music to get lost in melody and dancing. Sure, the world around us can burn, but can the sounds just stay on for the night? This isn't Nigerians playing ostrich. The pain is communal and endemic. Shared equally across socioeconomic divisions. Across social media and on the streets, everyone calls out in anger for improvement. And it's understood that the music won't heal us or usher in better days. Afrobeats will never make the pain go away, but it can make you feel good for a while.

In October 2020 the Nigerian military opened fire on unarmed protesters marching against police brutality at the Lekki toll gate in Lagos. The protest was

Opposite, from top to bottom: The singer Niniola performs at Gidifest in Lagos; Majek, an up-and-coming singer, performs at a Patoranking show in Abuja, while a young couple enjoys the music.

one of many demonstrations across the country at the time against police brutality. The demonstrators' anger was particularly trained on the Special Anti-Robbery Squad (SARS), a notoriously corrupt police unit. According to a report prepared by a panel investigating the massacre, at least twelve peaceful protesters were killed and dozens wounded. Four others were missing and 'presumed dead'. The 'atrocious maiming and killing of unarmed, helpless and unresisting protesters, while sitting on the floor and waving their Nigerian flags, while singing the national anthem can be equated to a "massacre" in context', said the report by the Lagos State Judicial Panel of Inquiry on Restitution for Victims of SARS-Related Abuses and Other Matters.

After the atrocities young Nigerians have used music to cope with and commemorate the event. Pop star Rema released a record, 'Peace of Mind', in which he references it, qualifying the general feeling as a collective 'pain'. Burna Boy's sombre addition, '20 10 20' – named for the date of the shooting – contains audio recordings from that night. But the real money-maker is Reekado Banks's 'Ozumba Mbadiwe', titled after the road on which the Lekki toll gate is located. The hit song, influenced heavily by South Africa's dancey amapiano genre, is a party song. Upbeat, with heavy drums and rolling synths, you'll be forgiven for not finding the connection to a massacre on first listen. But it's there in the lyrics, couched in symbolic language. But only if you can get past the groove. 'The song is feel-good and touches on societal problems and stuff,' explains Reekado Banks. In February 2022 Reekado released a remix, choosing to remove portions referencing the shooting for a more aspirational verse by the pop artist Fireboy DML.

And that's how Nigerians value music, for its escapist utility. Provide the groove. Provide the good feeling. Provide the aspirational lyrics. And, if you still have our attention, we'll probably listen to all the deep stuff you have to say. Music can still tell the Nigerian story, but can it do it on the dancefloor?

'I think it has not evolved beyond the surface, beyond the superficial,' says music producer Dunnie. One of the most diverse voices in Afrobeats, Dunnie started producing digital music in 2017 as a way to make ends meet. Plugged into the heart of the movement, she understands that Nigerian music utility has no pretension to depth. 'You want to go to clubs, you want to go to parties, and it gives you a good time. Afrobeats to us as Nigerians is an escape. There was a time when, if you make conscious music, people won't listen. It reminds them of their problems,' she says.

Who does today's music speak to? How does it tell the Nigerian story? What stories does it tell about the creators and the primary audience that it serves?

The music still tells the story of the people. At least a part of it. It takes snapshots of what it means to be Nigerian without the problems that plague that identity. Nigerian pop music examines the minutiae of human relationships, finding inventive ways to capture the nuances of human interaction. An emerging artist might lack electricity, experience difficulty while journeying to the studio, get stopped, harassed and extorted by corrupt police officers and struggle to eat. He'll complain to everyone around him until he gets into the recording booth. Once the mic is turned on, all his problems fall away. He'll most likely record a love song. Or an erotic one about the beauty of women's butts.

THE STARS

Yemi Alade: A hit factory and one-woman tower of Babel, who sings in English, Igbo, Pidgin, Yoruba, French, Swahili and Portuguese, so it'll come as no surprise that she has fans right across the continent. She is also an activist and UN Goodwill Ambassador.

Burna Boy: The grandson of Benson Idonije, former manager of Fela Kuti, with whom he shares a political and pan-African spirit. His hits are infused with reggae and dancehall sounds. In 2020 he won a Grammy for his album *Twice as Tall*.

Davido: Almost twenty-three million followers on Instagram, need we say more? Winner of MOBO, MTV Europe and BET musical awards, he has worked with Chris Brown and Meek Mill.

Sarz: The brains behind the hits of so many artists, including Wizkid, 2face Idibia and Niniola. His work as a producer has contributed to Afrobeats' international success.

Tiwa Savage: Queen of Afrobeats, style icon, winner of Best African Act at the 2018 MTV Europe Awards. She moved to London at the age of eleven and returned to Nigeria in 2012, attracted to the vibrancy of the music scene.

Wizkid: The leading Afrobeats export and Grammy winner, he has worked with artists such as Chris Brown, Future, Trey Songz and French Montana.

'Unlike film, music doesn't present a language barrier that can be fixed by subtitles. When Nigerian pop music crosses cultures and new markets, the actual words do not matter. What counts is the feeling.'

Look through all our charts, and romance dominates. Love is central to Nigerian music. It's the very foundation of Nigerian songwriting. A typical Nigerian hit explores the relationship between a man and woman. Whether as an exercise in romance or a lustful effort in scoring for the night or a heartbreak number for the people who have loved and lost, it's all narrated and delivered with rhythm and drumming. 'In life as a whole, we all just want to love and be loved by somebody. I don't really think that's one thing we are able to do in Nigeria,' says Ossi Grace, a songwriter with multiple credits on romantic records released by major labels. She continues, 'Especially women in Nigeria. We are taught to endure, we are not allowed to love ... it's something we claim, but we truly do not have it. If you're vulnerable, people look at you weird. You are supposed to be the hard guy.'

In Afrobeats all of that falls off. There are no judgements, no side stares, no snide remarks or expectations of modesty. If Wizkid sings about his heart-throb, you can co-opt his voice when the song is on and sing about yours. When Oxlade cries in solemn falsetto, he's allowed the space to be hurt, to be vulnerable, to find healing through his art. Music affords everyone that chance, side-stepping all the negatives that society places on it.

You can also find aspirational utility in the music. With eighty-three million people living in poverty in the country, survival is more than a word. It's life itself.

It's culture. It's why the average Nigerian is a hustler. Money has to be made daily. There are bills to be paid and enjoyment to be had. Money, or the appearance of it, is worshipped. And if you have more than enough just to get by, you can buy your way to and through anything. Afrobeats is a reflection of this. Music videos are mostly extravagant, swanky affairs in which the money never stops flowing, and the lifestyle is projected into every household.

The music soundtracks that element of society. Like Burna Boy's 2020 local hit 'Dangote'. Named after Nigerian billionaire and Africa's richest man, Aliko Dangote, the record questions the sense in slowing down and taking stock (see 'Aliko Dangote' on page 56). If the richest man in Africa wakes up daily and commutes to his office in search of more success, who then am I not to join in the race? Other versions of this 'hustle pop' include the plea for God's provision, the classic grass-to-grace tale and multiple diss tracks directed at haters. Poor, unrealised haters who are painted as antagonists and deserve to have their noses rubbed in the spectre of your success.

And that's why the music continues to resonate. It's escapist but carries the fundamental yearnings of the people. Afrobeats as a culture still tells the story, but one that's almost completely divorced from the past. It's a central unifier across Nigerians in every country or city. With Afrobeats taking on the world, these stories are hiding in plain sight. The

The Special Anti-Robbery Squad (SARS) was established in 1992 as an independent unit of the police to tackle the increase in violent crime and armed robbery in Nigerian cities. However, acting with impunity, it soon tarnished its reputation by carrying out the same offences it was supposed to prevent, if not worse: extortion, blackmail, home invasions, disappearances, torture, kidnappings and even organ trafficking, extrajudicial executions and rape. Tired of these crimes, citizens spoke out, especially after 2016, but their protests achieved little. The unit was investigated, and the government promised reforms, but nothing changed. An Amnesty International report documented eighty-two cases of summary executions committed by SARS between January 2017 and May 2020 alone. The turning point came with the circulation of a video on social media on 3 October 2020, in which special squad agents shot a man at a hotel in Ughelli, Delta State, then fled. Protests immediately resumed, reinvigorating the #EndSARS campaign, which had periodically been trending on Twitter. The movement, which soon gained a national dimension, was able to get the general police inspector to announce on 11 October that SARS would be disbanded. But who would guarantee that the promise would be kept this time? Protests did not stop, and neither did the clashes between #EndSARS and the forces of law and order, ending in the sad epilogue of the Lekki massacre, during which the Nigerian army fired on peaceful protestors who had gathered at a freeway toll booth on the outskirts of Lagos, killing at least twelve.

world doesn't connect with them now. Much of it is delivered in a language that takes some learning to decipher. But the sound is engaging and cuts across all of these barriers. Unlike film, music doesn't present a language barrier that can be fixed by subtitles. When Nigerian pop music crosses cultures and new markets, the actual words do not matter. What counts is the feeling or, as music enthusiasts say, 'the vibe'.

Across social media the sound continues to spread. On TikTok 'Ameno Amapiano Remix', a song by Nigerian rapper Goya Menor and Ghanaian producer Nektunez, has become a favourite across the world. 'You want to bam ba? You wanna chill with the big boys?' is a familiar tune across multiple continents. Fireboy DML celebrated another success with 'Peru', a collaboration with Ed Sheeran; it cracked the Billboard Hot 100, the world's most revered chart. There is talk of more Grammys in the future; Wizkid's 'Made in Lagos' was nominated for one in 2022.

'For me, music is from my soul. You can tell how I feel from my vocals. I think people can feel it as well,' says L.A.X. 'And that's why my music cuts across. Sometimes it's not about the music but the soul in the instrumentals and the voice behind the songs. African music is already taking over. I can see us performing at the biggest concerts in the world and also soundtracks for the biggest movies.'

He isn't lying. That future is already here. ✒

An Author Recommends

A film, a book and an album to understand Nigeria, chosen by:

NNAMDI EHIRIM

Nnamdi Ehirim a Nigerian entrepreneur and writer based in Lagos and Madrid. His debut novel, *Prince of Monkeys* (Counterpoint, 2019), follows the fortunes of a young, middle-class Lagosian and his friends in the latter years of the 20th century, covering topics such as politics, social class, spirituality and power – as well as featuring a cameo appearance by Fela Kuti. His essays, articles and short stories have appeared in *The Republic Journal*, *Afreada*, *Brittlepaper* and *The Kalahari Review*. As well as being a writer he is co-founder of a startup that aims to make sustainable energy more accessible in rural Nigeria.

THE FILM
OJUKOKORO
Dare Olaitan
2016

The Nigerian film industry, dubbed Nollywood, is one of the world's most prolific. During its rise to prominence in the 2000s, comedies and romance flicks set on university campuses or in small villages were blue-chip templates; entire movies were written, shot and made available for sale within weeks, and the production of multiple sequels was the rule not the exception. In recent times movie sets have transferred to more glamorous urban locations, but not much else has changed. Yet, with his first movie, *Ojukokoro*, a young director called Dare Olaitan decided to stray as far as he possibly could from the proven tropes of Nollywood success and instead chose to tell a more authentic version of Nigerian reality.

Ojukokoro is set almost exclusively in a run-down fuel station that serves more as a vehicle for laundering money than actually serving any vehicle. The station's manager is underpaid and cash-strapped, so he decides to rob the business. However, half the cast harbour similar intentions.

Ojukokoro is a Yoruba word that translates as 'greed'. Greed, in most cultures, is perceived as a vice. However, Olaitan's film holds a mirror to society and argues – with the help of an ensemble cast and sharp, witty dialogue – that when poverty thrives and scarcity means your fair share often amounts to nothing, greed evolves beyond a moral leaning and becomes a necessary tool for survival, to have means to take from someone else.

THE BOOK
HALF OF A YELLOW SUN
Chimamanda Ngozi Adichie
Harper Perennial, 2007 (USA) /
Fourth Estate, 2006 (UK)

Chimamanda Ngozi Adichie was only twenty-six years old when her debut novel *Purple Hibiscus* arrived on book-shelves in 2003. At the time, the two most prominent names in Nigerian litera-ture – Chinua Achebe and Wole Soyinka – were already in their sixties and seven-ties, and readers were more likely to encounter them in classrooms, because foreign fiction had become more popular with bookstores and street vendors. *Purple Hibiscus* appealed to an entire generation of youthful readers thirsty for stories about people similar to themselves who spoke to them like their friends. Adichie's immigrant tale *Americanah*, which was published a decade later, cemented her status as the literary icon of her generation. However, it's her second novel, *Half of a Yellow Sun*, a Nigerian Civil War epic set decades in the past, that stands out as her most ambitious and rewarding work.

The novel's stage spans the breadth of Nigeria's immense landscape, beginning in the university town of Nsukka, moving briefly to the affluence of Lagos and, at one point, exploring the centuries-old city of Kano. Its plot employs the most pivotal event in Nigeria's history – the two-and-a-half-year inter-ethnic civil war – as the backdrop for conversations on national identity, as a battleground for the eternal tussle of tradition versus modernity and as a stage for a stunning tragedy that leaves its heroes and hero-ines grieving the loss of family, lovers and friends.

THE ALBUM
MADE IN LAGOS
Wizkid
2021

In Nigeria some people say the easiest career path anyone can take is to become a DJ because there is such an abun-dance of good music constantly being produced, most of which is in a style called Afrobeats. It is largely inspired by the Afrobeat genre pioneered by Fela Kuti in the 1970s but with a modern twist. Ayodeji 'Wizkid' Balogun is arguably the genre's prime influencer. Since the release of his debut album in 2011 his music has received massive airplay across sub-Saharan Africa, and he has consistently sold out shows on every continent.

Wizkid's third studio album, *Made in Lagos*, is the most impressive case study of Afrobeat's reinvention. Although main-taining the same swinging tempo as Fela's prototype, Wizkid's songs are a lot shorter and less dependent on live instru-mental riffs. The vocal performances are still not contemporary-choirworthy, but Wizkid's melodies are as compelling as any Sunday-worship session. The beats are still made to be played at the loudest volume, while the rhythms still inspire sensual dancefloor moves. However, Wizkid's lyrics are a lot less politicised than his forebears' and a lot more centred on the extravagances of youth – simple, globally relatable rants on the pursuit of love, wealth and enjoyment. Beyond being a testament to the virtuosity of music from the African continent, the album also succeeds at building bridges with the Black diaspora from the Caribbean, North America and Europe through collabora-tions that borrow from the cultures of these distant relatives of ours.

The Playlist

SIMONE BERTUZZI/PALM WINE
Translated by Alan Thawley

You could write hundreds of pages on the timelines, shifts, levels and complexities of Nigerian music in recent decades, and you would still be nowhere near covering everything. Even if you were to focus only on very recent years, you would be faced with one of the most prolific and profitable recording industries anywhere in the world, a complex market boasting astronomical figures and therefore impossible to capture in fifteen or so tracks. Naija pop – also known by the controversial term Afrobeats – a sound that has been expanding out from Lagos to the rest of the world for a couple of decades, is now, to all intents and purposes, a shape-shifting international phenomenon. So, rather than setting out chronologies, this playlist is a kind of snapshot in time that includes tracks that were produced in Nigeria in the past couple of years but which also encapsulates a pan-African movement that intertwines Lagos with Johannesburg through the amapiano sound.

Amapiano is a seductive deep-house concoction built on percussive basslines with synth interludes that emerged a decade ago in the townships of Joburg before being assimilated and deconstructed in Nigeria. From there, through the diaspora effect, it has now become transnational. So without looking at amapiano as a Nigerian genre – it is essentially South African with house and kwaito in its genetic makeup – this selection sets out to capture the vibrant side-story of its transformation, which demonstrates the extent to which genres and styles can now exist and evolve in hit parades around the world. So the playlist juxtaposes South African producers and Nigerian stars such as Davido, Wizkid and Patoranking.

However, having said there's no chronological element to the list, we do, in fact, open with a 2010 recording (albeit not released until 2020), 'Never (Lagos Never Gonna Be the Same)', by Tony Allen – the Nigerian percussionist and pioneer of Afrobeat who worked with Fela Kuti – and Hugh Masekela, the legendary South African trumpeter. The track is a tribute to Kuti, sung by Masekela: *Lagos never gonna be the same, never, without Fela.*

1

Tony Allen
and Hugh Masekela
*Never (Lagos Never
Gonna Be the Same)*
2020

2

DJ Tarico, Burna
Boy feat. Preck &
Nelson Tivane
Yaba Buluku
2021

3

Kabza de Small,
Wizkid, Burna Boy,
Cassper Nyovest,
Madumane
Sponono
2020

4

Focalistic, Davido,
Vigro Deep
Ke Star (Remix)
2021

5

DJ Tunez, D3AN,
Onosz
Lullaby
2020

6

Rexxie, Mohbad
KPK (Ko Por Ke)
2020

7

Davido, Focalistic
Champion Sound
2021

8

DJ Kaywise, Phyno
High Way
2020

9

Falz, Niniola
Squander
2020

10

Patoranking
Nobody
2020

11

MachiinaSa
James Bond
2021

12

Zinoleesky
Kilofeshe
2020

13

Asake
Mr Money
2020

14

Fireboy DML
Peru
2021

15

Wande Coal
Come My Way
2021

Digging Deeper

FICTION

Ayòbámi Adébáyò
Stay with Me
Knopf, 2017 (USA)/Canongate, 2017 (UK)

Chimamanda Ngozi Adichie
Purple Hibiscus
Algonquin, 2003 (USA)/
Fourth Estate, 2004 (UK)

A. Igoni Barrett
Blackass
Graywolf, 2016 (USA)/
Chatto & Windus, 2015 (UK)

Oyinkan Braithwaite
My Sister the Serial Killer
Doubleday, 2018 (USA)/Atlantic, 2019 (UK)

Teju Cole
Every Day Is for the Thief
Random House, 2014 (USA)/
Faber and Faber, 2015 (UK)

Abi Daré
The Girl with the Louding Voice
Sceptre, 2020

Sarah Ladipo Manyika
Like a Mule Bringing Ice Cream to the Sun
Cassava Republic, 2017

Chigozie Obioma
An Orchestra of Minorities
Back Bay Books, 2019 (USA)/
Little, Brown, 2019 (UK)

Chinelo Okparanta
Happiness, Like Water
Mariner Books, 2013

Chibundu Onuzo
Welcome to Lagos
Faber and Faber, 2017

Cheluchi Onyemelukwe-Onuobia
The Son of the House
Dundurn Press, 2021 (Can/USA) /
Europa Editions, 2021 (UK)

Lola Shoneyin
The Secret Lives of the Four Wives (USA) /
The Secret Lives of Baba Segi's Wives (UK)
William Morrow, 2011 (USA)/Serpent's
Tail, 2020 (UK)

Wole Soyinka
*Chronicles from the Land of the
Happiest People on Earth*
Pantheon, 2021 (USA)/Bloomsbury,
2021 (UK)

NON-FICTION

Various authors
*Of This Our Country: Acclaimed
Nigerian Authors on the Home, Identity
and Culture that They Know*
The Borough Press, 2021

Chinua Achebe
*There Was a Country: A
Personal History of Biafra*
Penguin, 2012 (USA)/Allen Lane, 2012 (UK)

Yemisi Aribisala
Longthroat Memoirs: Soups, Sex and Nigerian Taste Buds
Cassava Republic, 2016

Emmanuel Iduma
A Stranger's Pose
Cassava Republic, 2018

Elnathan John
Be(com)ing Nigerian: A Guide
Cassava Republic, 2019

Barnaby Phillips
Loot: Britain and the Benin Bronzes
Oneworld, 2022 (revised edition)

Noo Saro-Wiwa
Looking for Transwonderland: Travels in Nigeria
Soft Skull, 2012 (USA) / Granta, 2013 (UK)

Max Siollun
What Britain Did to Nigeria: A Short History of Conquest and Rule
Hurst, 2021

Olufemi Vaughan
Religion and the Making of Nigeria
Duke University Press, 2016

Emily Witt
Nollywood: The Making of a Film Empire
Columbia Global Reports, 2017

PODCASTS AND ARTICLES

Allyn Gaeste
'Things Fall Apart'
The Atavist, February 2018

George Packer
'The Megacity'
The New Yorker, 13 November 2006

Andrew Rice
'A Scorsese in Lagos'
The New York Times, 24 February 2012

Maite Vermeulen and Jacco Prantl
'NEPA: Never Expect Power Always'
De Correspondent, 2020

Graphic design and art direction:
Tomo Tomo and Pietro Buffa

Photography: Etinosa Yvonne
Photographic content curated by Prospekt Photographers

Illustrations: Edoardo Massa

Infographics and cartography: Pietro Buffa

Managing editor (English-language edition): Simon Smith

Thanks to: A. Igoni Barrett, Shaul Bassi, Lucia Boi, Alessandra Di Maio, Isabella Ferretti, Alessandro Foggetta, Gioia Guerzoni, Maaza Mengiste, Cheluchi Onyemelukwe, Chiara Piaggio, Lola Shoneyin, Maite Vermeulen, Frank Westerman

The opinions expressed in this publication are those of the authors and do not purport to reflect the views and opinions of the publishers. All content not specifically credited was written by The Passenger.

http://europaeditions.com/thepassenger
http://europaeditions.co.uk/thepassenger
#ThePassengerMag

The Passenger – Nigeria
© Iperborea S.r.l., Milan, and Europa Editions, 2023

Translators: Dutch — Emma Rault ('The Do-It-Yourself Society'), Diane Schaap ('Those Who Stay Behind'); Italian — Alan Thawley

Translations © Iperborea S.r.l., Milan, and Europa Editions, 2023, except 'Those Who Stay Behind' © Diane Schaap, 2019

ISBN 9781787704558

Printed on Munken Pure thanks to the support of Arctic Paper Printed by ELCOGRAF S.p.A., Verona, Italy